ECONOMIC POLICY IN THE REAGAN YEARS

ECONOMIC POLICY IN THE REAGAN YEARS

Charles F. Stone
and
Isabel V. Sawhill

The Changing Domestic Priorities Series

John L. Palmer and Isabel V. Sawhill, Editors

 THE URBAN INSTITUTE PRESS·WASHINGTON, D.C.

Copyright © 1984
THE URBAN INSTITUTE
2100 M Street, N.W.
Washington, D.C. 20037

Library of Congress Cataloging in Publication Data

Stone, Charles F.
  Economic policy in the Reagan years.

  (Changing domestic priorities series)
1. United States—Economic policy—1981—
I. Sawhill, Isabel V.   II. Title.   III. Series
HC106.8.S76   1984   338.973   84-27119
ISBN 0-87766-376-9 (cloth)
ISBN 0-87766-372-6 (pbk.)

Printed in the United States of America

9 8 7 6 5 4 3 2 1

THE URBAN INSTITUTE is a nonprofit policy research and educational organization established in Washington, D.C., in 1968. Its staff investigates the social and economic problems confronting the nation and government policies and programs designed to alleviate such problems. The Institute disseminates significant findings of its research through the publications program of its Press. The Institute has two goals for work in each of its research areas: to help shape thinking about societal problems and efforts to solve them, and to improve government decisions and performance by providing better information and analytic tools.

Through work that ranges from broad conceptual studies to administrative and technical assistance, Institute researchers contribute to the stock of knowledge available to public officials and to private individuals and groups concerned with formulating and implementing more efficient and effective government policy.

Conclusions or opinions expressed in Institute publications are those of the authors and do not necessarily reflect the views of other staff members, officers or trustees of the Institute, advisory groups, or any organizations which provide financial support to the Institute.

The Changing Domestic Priorities Series

Listed below are the titles available, or soon to be available, in the Changing Domestic Priorities Series

Books

THE REAGAN EXPERIMENT
An Examination of Economic and Social Policies under the Reagan Administration (1982), John L. Palmer and Isabel V. Sawhill, editors

HOUSING ASSISTANCE FOR OLDER AMERICANS
The Reagan Prescription (1982), James P. Zais, Raymond J. Struyk, and Thomas Thibodeau

MEDICAID IN THE REAGAN ERA
Federal Policy and State Choices (1982), Randall R. Bovbjerg and John Holahan

WAGE INFLATION
Prospects for Deceleration (1983), Wayne Vroman

OLDER AMERICANS IN THE REAGAN ERA
Impacts of Federal Policy Changes (1983), James R. Storey

FEDERAL HOUSING POLICY AT PRESIDENT REAGAN'S MIDTERM
(1983), Raymond J. Struyk, Neil Mayer, and John A. Tuccillo

STATE AND LOCAL FISCAL RELATIONS IN THE EARLY 1980s
(1983), Steven D. Gold

THE DEFICIT DILEMMA
Budget Policy in the Reagan Era (1983), Gregory B. Mills and John L. Palmer

HOUSING FINANCE
A Changing System in the Reagan Era (1983), John A. Tuccillo with John L. Goodman, Jr.

PUBLIC OPINION DURING THE REAGAN ADMINISTRATION
National Issues, Private Concerns (1983), John L. Goodman, Jr.

RELIEF OR REFORM?
Reagan's Regulatory Dilemma (1984), George C. Eads and Michael Fix

THE REAGAN RECORD
An Assessment of America's Changing Domestic Priorities (1984), John L. Palmer and Isabel V. Sawhill, editors (Ballinger Publishing Co.)

Conference Volumes

THE SOCIAL CONTRACT REVISITED
  Aims and Outcomes of President Reagan's Social Welfare Policy (1984), edited
  by D. Lee Bawden
NATURAL RESOURCES AND THE ENVIRONMENT
  The Reagan Approach (1984), edited by Paul R. Portney
FEDERAL BUDGET POLICY IN THE 1980s (1984), edited by
  Gregory B. Mills and John L. Palmer
THE REAGAN REGULATORY STRATEGY
  An Assessment (1984), edited by George C. Eads and Michael Fix
THE LEGACY OF REAGANOMICS
  Prospects for Long-term Growth (1984), edited by Charles R. Hulten and Isabel
  V. Sawhill
THE REAGAN PRESIDENCY AND THE GOVERNING OF AMERICA
  (1984), edited by Lester M. Salamon and Michael S. Lund

Advisory Board of the
Changing Domestic Priorities Project

CONTENTS

TABLES

FIGURES

FOREWORD

This book is part of The Urban Institute's Changing Domestic Priorities project. The project is examining changes that are occurring in the nation's domestic policies under the Reagan administration and is analyzing the effects of those changes on people, places, and institutions.

The Reagan administration's economic objectives were to curb inflation, reduce unemployment, and increase long-term growth. Such objectives were hardly controversial, but the weight given to different objectives and the mix of policies used to achieve these objectives was. The administration tolerated a deep recession as the cost of reducing inflation; and its endorsement of a combination of supply-side tax cuts and slow growth in the money supply put fiscal and monetary policy on a collision course and left enormous budget deficits as the principal legacy.

Although unconventional, in many respects the administration's program appears to have been successful. Inflation has declined to its lowest level in over a decade and, as of late 1984, the economy was growing strongly. However, the prospects for continued growth are clouded by the large deficits currently projected for the late 1980s.

This volume addresses a number of issues: How much of the decline in inflation is attributable to administration policies and how much would probably have occurred whoever had been president? What caused the recession of 1981–1982 and the subsequent recovery? Would an alternative set of economic policies have improved economic performance in the first half of the decade? And what are the prospects for the remainder of the decade? In particular, will the rate of economic growth be higher or lower as the result of President Reagan's policies?

The book's major findings are summarized in the introduction to this volume and also in chapter 3 of *The Reagan Record*. While the findings will be of obvious interest to professional economists, the authors have placed a premium on keeping the material accessible to students and non-economists as well, on the theory that economic literacy is a public good currently in short supply.

John L. Palmer
Isabel V. Sawhill
Editors
Changing Domestic Priorities Series

ACKNOWLEDGMENTS

We would like to thank Cathy Cromer and Mary Kate Smith for their valuable research assistance and Lisa Burns and Ann Guillot for their skill and patience in the typing and preparation of the manuscript. We would also like to acknowledge the assistance with the DRI simulations provided by Eric Dressler and the comments on earlier drafts provided by Robert Solow, Herbert Stein, and James Tobin—without, of course, holding them responsible for the final product. Finally we would like to thank the Ford Foundation and the John D. and Catherine T. MacArthur Foundation for their financial support.

ABOUT THE AUTHORS

Charles F. Stone is a research associate at The Urban Institute, working on the Changing Domestic Priorities project. His current research interests include macroeconomic and budget policy. He has worked as an economist at the Federal Trade Commission and at the Office of Economic Policy of the Office of Management and Budget, and was a staff member of the Review Panel on New Drug Regulation in the U.S. Department of Health, Education, and Welfare. He has also taught extensively, most recently at Swarthmore College. He is a contributing author of *The Reagan Record*.

Isabel V. Sawhill is codirector of The Urban Institute's Changing Domestic Priorities project. Dr. Sawhill's areas of research include human resources and economic policy. She has directed several of the Institute's research programs and held a number of government positions, including that of director of the National Commission for Employment Policy. Her publications include *Youth Employment and Public Policy*; *Time of Transition: The Growth of Families Headed by Women*; *The Reagan Experiment*; *The Legacy of Reaganomics: Prospects for Long-Term Growth*; and *The Reagan Record*.

INTRODUCTION

The economy that Ronald Reagan inherited had been performing poorly for a number of years. Compared with the prosperous 1960s, the 1970s were years of high inflation and sluggish economic growth, with most measures of material well-being showing only modest increases. President Reagan blamed the misguided policies of previous administrations for this poor performance and forecast that adoption of the tax cuts, spending restraint, regulatory relief, and monetary discipline embodied in his Program for Economic Recovery would, by reversing these policies, rapidly and painlessly restore sustained noninflationary growth.

In arguing for tax cuts, spending restraint, and regulatory relief, the administration embraced the supply-side view that the sluggish growth of the 1970s was due chiefly to the growing size and intrusiveness of the federal government. The key to improving the economy's long-term growth prospects lay therefore in limiting the scope of government and expanding the private sector. In arguing for monetary restraint, the administration embraced the monetarist view that the high inflation and high unemployment of the 1970s resulted from misguided attempts to manipulate aggregate demand through discretionary changes in monetary and fiscal policy. The key to achieving high employment with reasonable price stability lay therefore in stable money growth. In arguing that a decline in inflation and unemployment could be achieved simultaneously, the administration embraced the rational expectations view that a credible commitment to controlling inflation could quickly dissipate inflationary expectations without the need for a recession or even a slowing of economic growth.

Each of these positions was controversial. Most economists recognized that tax cuts could, in principle, encourage work effort, saving, and investment and thus the economy's capacity to supply goods and services;

1

but many doubted that the effects would be as large as the supply-siders seemed to think. Most economists also recognized that erratic macro-economic policies could be destabilizing, but many believed that the high inflation and unemployment of the 1970s had as much to do with the economy's having to adjust to a number of shocks—most notably two oil price shocks—as it did with "stop-and-go" monetary and fiscal policies. Finally, most economists recognized that slower monetary growth was necessary to bring down inflation, but many believed that inflationary expectations had become so embedded in the economy by 1980 that the costs of lowering inflation through monetary restraint could be high in terms of lost output and employment.

In contrast to the optimism inherent in the president's economic recovery program, mainstream economists offered only an unpleasant choice between risking still greater inflation by pursuing more rapid growth and enduring slower growth in order to make grudging progress against inflation. It is perhaps not surprising, therefore, that the country chose to experiment with economic policies that promised better outcomes.

One important result of that choice has been a remarkably rapid decline in the rate of inflation; but success against inflation has been accompanied by a severe recession, high interest rates, large budget deficits, and an exceptionally strong dollar. Although the Reagan experiment in macro-economic policy may yet end up producing a healthier and more prosperous economy than what could have been achieved by a more conventional set of policies, its promise of a painless victory over inflation was not realized. Moreover, unless the problem of the budget deficits is solved, the program's prospects for long-term success are clouded by the threat of persistently high interest rates or renewed inflation.

Our goals in this study of economic policy in the Reagan years are to document and analyze the results achieved so far and to assess the likely longer-run consequences of these policies. The findings and conclusions that are developed in greater detail in subsequent chapters are summarized here.

- The decline in inflation from 1980 to 1983 was indeed substantial, but inflationary forces were amplified in 1979 and 1980 by a number of unfavorable price shocks and they were attenuated after 1980 by a number of favorable movements in food, energy, and import prices. This change from unfavorable shocks to favorable price movements explains between one-third and one-half of the decline in inflation between 1980 and 1983.
- The permanent decline of about five points in the underlying rate of inflation that the economy will have realized once high employment

is restored is not out of line with what might have been expected from mainstream models of the inflation process. There is no evidence that inflation has fallen more rapidly as a result of any rational expectations or credibility effects—that is, inflation has declined largely because unemployment was high.

- The fight against inflation that began in 1980 will end up costing the economy about $1 trillion in lost output (measured in constant 1982 dollars) by the time the economy returns to high employment.
- The budget and tax changes of 1981 and 1982 and the subsequent emergence of large budget deficits that most people view as the defining feature of the Reagan administration's economic policy are less important to understanding what happened to the economy between 1981 and 1984 than is the conduct of monetary policy. It was the Federal Reserve Board's commitment to fighting inflation by closely controlling the rate of growth of the money supply that shaped economic events over this period. Although the Fed's behavior was broadly consistent with the desires of the Reagan administration, the course of monetary policy was set before Ronald Reagan was elected president and might well have been pursued whatever the outcome of the election.
- In retrospect, this period was a bad time to pursue a monetarist strategy of trying to control the money supply, because the relationship between changes in the money supply and changes in national income—the so-called velocity of money—was highly unstable and unpredictable. Although the Fed demonstrated some flexibility in its control of money growth, it failed to adjust quickly enough to the surge in money demand that produced an unprecedented decline in velocity in 1982. As a result, spending slowed drastically and the recession was deeper than it would have been if the Fed had been more accommodating toward people's increased demand for money.
- Given the Fed's commitment to lowering inflation between 1979 and 1983, changes in fiscal policy probably could have done little that would have significantly altered the growth path of national income in the short run. The additional stimulus provided by the Reagan administration's fiscal policies (an increase in the standardized budget deficit of about 2 percent of GNP, compared with a fiscal policy more like that of the 1970s) had some effect in moderating the effects of tight money, but the major effect of the clash between tight monetary and loose fiscal policies was to raise interest rates and alter the composition of output. Business tax cuts offset the effects of high interest rates on business plant and equipment spending, but consumption is higher and residential investment

and net exports are lower under the Reagan administration's fiscal policies.

- Some of the costs associated with the recession could have been avoided by tolerating a smaller decline in inflation. If a policy mix more like that of the 1970s had been followed, with tighter fiscal policy, looser monetary policy, and less overall restraint than the policies we actually followed, there still would have been a recession, but it would have been milder (with output losses roughly half those actually experienced). Inflation would still have fallen but it would have been higher than the rate actually experienced by 1984. Structural deficits would have been virtually eliminated, easing the burden on housing and net exports and removing a major source of uncertainty about the future.

- The economy's long-term growth prospects were improved as a result of the tax cuts, spending cuts, and regulatory relief enacted as part of the president's economic recovery program. However, the lower capital formation associated with the recession and the high interest rates associated with large budget deficits have probably worked in the other direction. Putting reasonable bounds on the quantitative magnitudes of these counterbalancing effects suggests that the economic policies of the Reagan years are unlikely to end up raising real output in 1990 by more than 4 to 5 percent above what it would have been without these policies, even if we assume, optimistically, that the supply-side effects are relatively large and there is relatively little crowding out of investment by large budget deficits. Alternatively, these policies are unlikely to lower real output by more than 3 to 4 percent, even if we assume, pessimistically, that the supply-side effects are relatively weak and there is substantial crowding out of investment. Most likely, these effects will roughly offset one another, leaving the economy's long-term real growth path much as it would have been if more conventional macroeconomic policies had been followed.

CHAPTER 1

THE FIGHT AGAINST INFLATION

The primary goal of the Reagan administration's economic recovery program was to restore the long-term health and vitality of the economy, but the program held out the promise of a quick improvement in short-term performance as well. The administration forecast that if its policies were followed, the economy would immediately experience a decline in inflation and healthy real growth. More conventional forecasts were less optimistic than the administration's, both about how much inflation would come down and about how rapidly the economy would grow.[1]

Figure 1 shows that the Reagan administration's forecast and the more conventional forecast of the Congressional Budget Office (CBO) missed the mark in important respects. Between 1980 and 1983 inflation declined even more than the administration had forecast, but the magnitude of the rise in unemployment and the decline in real output were not anticipated, even in the more pessimistic CBO forecast. In this chapter we examine the substantial decline in inflation that was the main positive economic development in the first years of the Reagan presidency, and we assess the costs paid by the economy in achieving these gains against inflation.

The Reagan Prescription

Candidate Reagan had been highly successful in exploiting the widespread public perception that the economy was in worse shape in 1980 than it had been four years earlier, and in many respects it was. After three

---

1. For the administration's economic assumptions, see *America's New Beginning, A Program for Economic Recovery* (Washington, D.C.: Government Printing Office, February 18, 1981), Part III, p. S-1. For a more conventional forecast, see the Congressional Budget Office, *An Analysis of President Reagan's Budget Revisions for Fiscal Year 1982* (Washington, D.C.: Government Printing Office, March 1981), p. 4.

FIGURE 1
FORECAST COMPARISONS

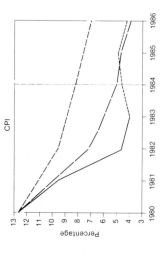

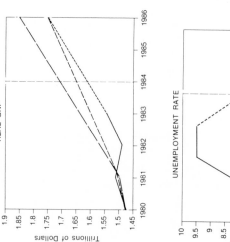

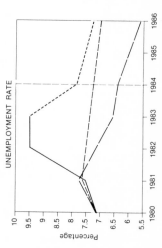

---------- Congressional Budget Office forecast, March 1981
———— Administration forecast, February 1981
———— Actual
·········· Administration forecast, January 1984

SOURCES: The White House, *America's New Beginning: A Program for Economic Recovery*, Part III (Washington, D.C.: February 18, 1981), p. S-1; Office of Management and Budget, *Budget of the United States Government, Fiscal Year 1985* (Washington, D.C.: Government Printing Office, 1984), pp. 210–211; and Congressional Budget Office, *Analysis of President Reagan's Budget Revisions for Fiscal Year 1982* (Washington, D.C.: Government Printing Office, 1981), p. 4.

years of strong economic growth and rising family incomes from 1976 to 1978, the economy was hit in 1979 by its second oil price shock in less than a decade. The drain of these higher oil prices on consumer purchasing power, together with restrictive monetary and fiscal policies designed to prevent a further rise in inflation, caused a brief recession in 1980. Unemployment, which had hovered just below the 6 percent rate generally accepted as high employment throughout 1979, rose above 7 percent in 1980, yet consumer prices continued to rise at double-digit rates. By some measures, the average family's real income was lower in 1980 than it had been in 1976.[2]

This experience capped a decade of disappointing economic performance in which rising inflation was accompanied by flagging economic growth and high unemployment. Figure 2 shows that the average inflation and unemployment rates rose during the 1970s, but it also shows that both displayed considerable cyclical variability. In general, periods of falling inflation were also periods of relatively high unemployment, whereas periods of falling unemployment were generally periods of rising inflation.

The Reagan administration attributed the unfortunate combination of rising unemployment and inflation experienced during the 1970s to stop-and-go monetary and fiscal policies that alternated between periods of excessive stimulus, which increased inflationary pressures, and periods of short-lived restraint, which raised unemployment without having much effect on inflation. The administration argued that people had no incentive to abandon inflationary behavior in such a policy environment, but that once it had become clear that policymakers did not intend to abandon their anti-inflation efforts at the first sign of rising unemployment, people would be encouraged to lower their wage and price demands in anticipation of greater price stability. According to this "rational expectations" view, inflation could fall rapidly without there being any loss in output or employment growth. The administration argued further that its supply-side tax and spending cuts were different from the Keynesian policies of the past in that they would encourage the supply of additional output and stimulate economic growth, rather than simply add to the demand for existing output. With supply increasing in line with demand, there would be little or no upward pressure on prices.

---

2. Using the Consumer Price Index (CPI) to measure inflation, real median family income (in 1982 dollars) rose from $25,363 in 1976 to $26,047 in 1979 but then fell back to $24,626 in 1980. Using the Personal Consumption Expenditure (PCE) deflator, average real income was higher in 1980 than in 1976. See pages 12–16 for a discussion of the differences in these indexes. Real per capita disposable income also was higher in 1980 than it had been in 1976.

FIGURE 2

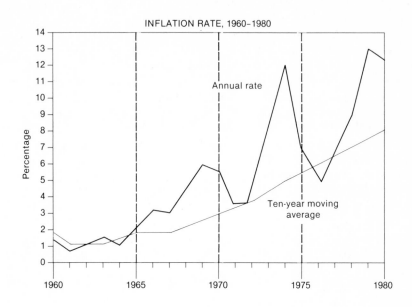

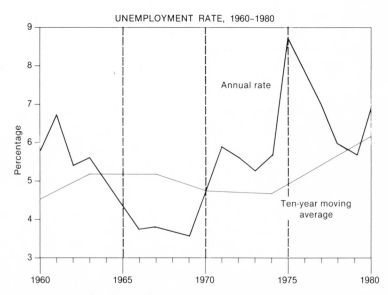

SOURCE: Consumer Price Index for all urban consumers and civilian unemployment rate from the U.S. Department of Labor, Bureau of Labor Statistics (BLS).

Thus, the administration's forecast of a painless victory over inflation was predicated on rational expectations and supply-side propositions—and a belief that past inflation and unemployment could both have been lower if different policies had been followed. These views were not shared, however, by mainstream economists whose analysis of the economy's experience with inflation and unemployment since the mid-1960s was quite different from the administration's analysis.

The Mainstream View: An Inflation-Unemployment Dilemma

The origins of the double-digit inflation of 1979 and 1980 can be traced to the 1965–1968 period, when President Johnson attempted to finance both the Vietnam War and the Great Society without raising taxes.[3] Many economists believed at the time that such a policy was ill-advised, and the inflation it produced was no surprise. The surprise was that inflation hardly fell at all when unemployment rose in response to the restrictive policies introduced in 1969. After nearly a decade of expansion (from the first quarter of 1961 to the fourth quarter of 1969, according to the National Bureau of Economic Research), the economy went into a recession in 1970, yet inflation remained at about 5 percent. Unwilling to endure the deeper recession that would have been required to eliminate the inflationary expectations and behavior that had taken hold during the long expansion, President Nixon in 1971 responded to the unemployment by restimulating the economy and to the inflation by instituting wage and price controls. Most analysts believe that controls merely repressed inflation for a time, and some believe that they actually aggravated the inflation that reemerged when controls were later relaxed.[4]

This account of macroeconomic policy through the early 1970s is broadly consistent with the Reagan administration's critique of past policy and performance, but that critique fits events after 1973 less well. In 1973 and 1974 and again in 1979 and 1980, the world economy was rocked by substantial oil and other commodity price increases. The need to pay higher oil prices reduced real incomes in the United States and other oil-

---

3. For a detailed analysis of the rise of inflation and unemployment in the 1970s, see Gary H. Jefferson, "Inflation and Unemployment in the 1970s: Structural Change or Policy-Induced?" Changing Domestic Priorities Discussion Paper (Washington, D.C.: The Urban Institute, June 1984).

4. A. S. Blinder and W. J. Newton, "The 1971–74 Control Program and the Price Level: An Econometric Post-Mortem," *Journal of Monetary Economics*, vol. 8, no. 1 (July 1981), pp. 1–23.

consuming countries. Policymakers faced a dilemma. If they tried to cushion the short-run effects of these price shocks with expansionary monetary
and fiscal policies, they risked inflation and a delay in the economy's adjustment to higher real oil prices and lower real incomes. But if they attempted to extinguish the inflation generated by these oil shocks with restrictive monetary and fiscal policies, they risked recession and
unemployment.

Policy did indeed swing back and forth between stimulus, when unemployment seemed the greater evil, and restraint, when inflation seemed
the greater evil. Given the shocks the economy was experiencing, however,
it is not clear that different policies would have produced better outcomes
than did these stop-and-go policies. The nation probably had no choice but
to adjust to more expensive oil, either by keeping the inflation rate down
and accepting higher unemployment during the period of adjustment or
by keeping unemployment down and accepting higher inflation. Policymakers at the time chose to accept some of each. In retrospect, some, including President Reagan, may think a different path should have been
followed; but it is very unlikely that any policy could have achieved both
lower inflation *and* lower unemployment.

According to this interpretation, the inflation and unemployment
that Ronald Reagan inherited were not simply the legacy of a decade of
unrestrained and excessively stimulative policies, but also the legacy of a
world oil crisis that had already reduced American living standards and
whose inflationary consequences would require still further adjustments in
the early 1980s. Accepting this analysis, many mainstream economists offered only unpleasant choices in their policy prescriptions. Most believed
that restraining the growth of aggregate demand was a necessary condition
for lowering inflation, but they also believed that the restrictive policies
necessary to restrain demand would probably produce losses in output and
employment along with a decline in inflation. Thus, policymakers faced a
choice among accepting inflation, accepting the output costs associated
with lowering inflation, or pursuing incomes policies of one sort or another—that is, some direct actions to moderate wage and price increases—
despite their questionable effectiveness in the past.

Keynesians were particularly pessimistic about the output costs of
lowering inflation. Econometric studies of the relationship between inflation and unemployment indicated to them that inflation would come down
only slowly even in the face of substantial economic slack. Based on these
studies, Arthur Okun concluded, for example, that each point of unemployment in excess of high employment maintained for a year would lower
the inflation rate by between 0.17 and 0.5 points, with an average expected

effect of 0.3 points.[5] By this calculation, economic slack equivalent to ten years of 9 percent unemployment was required to eliminate ten points of inflation. Monetarists were generally less specific about how the slower growth in nominal income brought about by tighter money would be split between slower growth in output and lower inflation, but few believed that monetary restraint could reduce inflation without causing any short-run losses in output and employment.

As we have seen, neither this pessimism nor the optimism of the Reagan administration was fully borne out by the behavior of the economy between 1980 and 1983. In the face of about ten "point years" of excess unemployment during this period, the Consumer Price Index (CPI) dropped almost nine points, and other measures of inflation declined sharply as well (table 1). The economic slack associated with this decline in inflation has been much greater than what the Reagan administration predicted, but the decline in inflation has been much greater than what would have been predicted on the basis of the Okun estimate of the effect of eco-

TABLE 1

MEASURES OF INFLATION, 1976-1983
(Percentage change)

Year	Consumer Price Index[a]	GNP Deflator[b]	Producer Price Index[c]	Employment Cost Index[d]	Productivity- Adjusted Compensation[e]
1976	4.8	4.7	3.7	7.2	6.2
1977	6.8	6.1	6.9	7.0	5.0
1978	9.0	8.5	9.2	7.6	8.5
1979	13.3	8.2	12.8	8.7	11.3
1980	12.4	10.2	11.8	9.0	10.6
1981	8.9	8.7	7.1	8.8	7.9
1982	3.9	4.4	3.7	6.3	6.3
1983	3.8	4.1	0.6	5.0	1.4

a. CPI for all urban consumers, December to December. SOURCE: U.S. Department of Labor, BLS.

b. Fourth quarter to fourth quarter. SOURCE: U.S. Department of Commerce, Bureau of Economic Analysis (BEA).

c. Finished goods index, December to December. SOURCE: BLS.

d. Fourth quarter to fourth quarter. SOURCE: BLS.

e. Compensation per hour less output per hour in the nonfarm business sector, fourth quarter to fourth quarter. SOURCE: BEA.

5. Arthur Okun, "Efficient Disinflationary Policies," *American Economic Review*, vol. 68, no. 3 (May 1978), pp. 348-352.

nomic slack. Although this rapid decline in inflation seems to support the rational expectations view that past estimates of the output costs of lowering inflation were unduly pessimistic, an examination of the causes of the decline in inflation shows that the permanent decline in inflation that will be realized once the economy returns to high employment is likely to be consistent with the Okun estimate.

Why Inflation Fell

Table 1 shows the behavior of several measures of inflation between 1976 and 1983. Among regularly published measures of inflation, the most widely followed are the CPI and the implicit price deflator for the gross national product (GNP). The former is a measure of price changes for goods and services typically bought by urban consumers, who represent 80 percent of the population. The latter covers a broader class of goods and services and provides the most comprehensive measure of general price inflation. By either measure, inflation rose through 1980 and declined thereafter, although the decline in the CPI was 8.6 points and the decline in the GNP deflator was only 6.1 points. The other measures of inflation reported in table 1 are measures of input cost inflation. The Producer Price Index (PPI) measures changes in prices charged to sellers, which foreshadow changes in consumer prices. The employment cost index and the productivity-corrected compensation per hour index are measures of labor costs, the most important element in overall costs. The former measures wage increases and the latter measures the upward pressure on product prices from wage increases in excess of productivity growth.

Measurement Error

Most people worry about inflation because of its impact on their purchasing power as consumers, hence the attention given to the CPI. Until 1983, however, the CPI was a flawed measure of inflation because it exaggerated the importance of mortgage interest rates and other homeownership costs and was overly sensitive to their sometimes volatile movements.[6] A better measure of inflation was probably one of the Personal Consump-

---

6. For a detailed discussion of the problems with the CPI, see Executive Office of the President, Council of Economic Advisers, Office of Management and Budget, *Report on Indexing Federal Programs* (Washington, D.C.: Government Printing Office, January 1981); and A. S. Blinder, "The Consumer Price Index and the Measurement of Recent Inflation," *Brookings Papers on Economic Activity*, 1980:2, pp. 539–573.

tion Expenditure (PCE) price indexes from the National Income and Product Accounts (NIA).[7] These measure a broader sample of consumer expenditures and have consistently measured homeownership costs in a conceptually more appealing manner than has the CPI. In 1983, however, the treatment of homeownership costs in the CPI was improved, so the CPI and the PCE indexes can be expected to move similarly from now on.

Because of its previous problems, the CPI tended to overstate inflation when mortgage interest rates and other homeownership costs were rising and to understate inflation when they were falling. This excessive volatility of the CPI is illustrated in figure 3 and table 2, which compare annual rates of change in the CPI, the fixed-weight PCE index, and the CPI-X-1, an experimental CPI published for a time along with the official CPI whose treatment of homeownership costs was similar to that of the PCE indexes and to the official CPI as it is now calculated. These data show that the CPI tended to overstate inflation before 1981 but to understate it in 1982. Over the whole period, both the PCE index and the CPI-X-1 moved more closely with one another than either moved with the official CPI.

While inflation as measured by the official CPI was 12.4 percent in 1980, the inflation experienced by the average household was closer to the 10.8 percent registered by the CPI-X-1. Thus, 1.6 points of the decline in inflation registered by the CPI between 1980 and 1983 would have occurred simply as a result of the change in measurement procedures implemented in 1983, even if all the underlying prices had continued to increase at the same rate. In other words, nearly 20 percent of the decline in inflation measured by the CPI simply reflected earlier measurement errors.

Nevertheless, the rate of inflation, satisfactorily measured, fell by nearly two-thirds in only three years. Both the CPI-X-1 and the fixed-weight PCE rates of inflation fell 7 points, from just under 11 percent per year to just under 4 percent per year. It is this seven-point drop in inflation that needs to be explained.

---

7. Three PCE price indexes are published. The implicit PCE deflator measures the ratio of the current value of personal consumption expenditures to their value when measured in base-year prices. The base year is currently 1972. Unfortunately, changes in the PCE deflator confound changes in prices and changes in quantities, because there are no fixed weights in year-to-year calculations of the index. The fixed-weight PCE price index avoids this problem by measuring price changes for a fixed marketbasket of goods, currently 1972 personal consumption expenditures. Its method of calculation is comparable to that for the CPI, and it shares with the CPI the problem that over time the base-period marketbasket can become unrepresentative of current consumer expenditure patterns. The chain-weighted PCE index solves this problem by continually updating the expenditure weights to those of the previous period's expenditure patterns. Despite their disparate methods of calculation, all three indexes can generally be expected to move together.

FIGURE 3

ALTERNATIVE MEASURES
OF CONSUMER PRICE INFLATION, 1976–1983

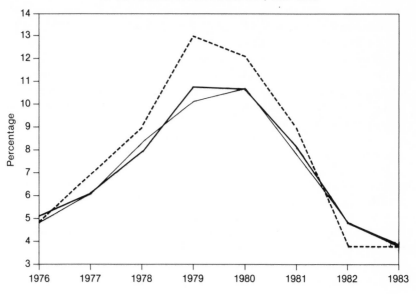

---------- CPI (all urban consumers), December to December
———————— Fixed-weight Personal Consumption Expenditure price index
———————— CPI-X-1

SOURCES: BLS and BEA.

Food, Energy, and Import Prices

Conceptually, inflation is a general increase in prices, but it is measured as a weighted average of individual price changes. From time to time price changes peculiar to individual markets can be large enough to disguise the impact of monetary and fiscal policy on the underlying general rate of inflation. The effect of volatile homeownership costs on the CPI is an example.

In a similar fashion, food and energy prices have been more volatile in recent years than prices generally (see table 3[8]). If the effects of these vola-

---

8. The calculations in table 3 are based on the fixed-weight PCE deflator, because specialized indexes for the CPI-X-1 are not readily available. If they were, it is unlikely that they would deviate significantly from those for the PCE index.

TABLE 2

ALTERNATIVE MEASURES OF CONSUMER PRICE INFLATION, 1976–1983
(*Percentage change*)

Year	CPI[a]	PCE[b]	CPI-X-1[a]
1976	4.8	4.8	5.1
1977	6.8	6.3	6.3
1978	9.0	8.5	7.9
1979	13.3	10.3	10.8
1980	12.4	10.9	10.8
1981	8.9	8.1	8.5
1982	3.9	5.0	5.0
1983	3.8	3.8	3.8[c]

a. All urban consumers, December to December. SOURCE: BLS. The CPI-X-1 was discontinued after 1982 with the change in the official CPI (see text).

b. Fourth-quarter-to-fourth-quarter change in the fixed-weight PCE index. SOURCE: BEA.

c. Change in official CPI.

TABLE 3

REMOVING VOLATILE COMPONENTS FROM THE FIXED-WEIGHT PERSONAL
CONSUMPTION EXPENDITURE PRICE INDEX
(*Percentage change, fourth quarter to fourth quarter*)

Year	Fixed-Weight Indexes					
	PCE	Food	Energy	Nonoil PCE Imports	PCE Less Food and Energy	PCE Less Food, Energy, and Imports[a]
1976	4.8	0.4	5.2	6.5	6.3	6.3
1977	6.3	5.9	7.8	9.5	6.4	6.1
1978	8.5	11.8	7.4	10.1	7.6	7.3
1979	10.3	8.8	37.4	12.0	7.4	6.9
1980	10.9	10.3	19.7	9.7	9.7	9.7
1981	8.1	4.9	12.5	−1.0	8.5	9.6
1982	5.0	3.2	2.2	−1.9	6.1	7.0
1983	3.8	2.4	−0.7	0.5	4.9	5.4

SOURCE: BEA and authors' calculations.

a. In 1980, nonoil PCE imports (M) accounted for about 10 percent of PCE less food (F) and energy (E). The "PCE less food, energy, and imports" change was calculated according to this formula: PCE (less FEM) = (PCE (less FE) − 0.1 M) ÷ 0.9.

tile food and energy prices were removed by, in effect, assuming that they increased in line with other prices, the rise in inflation through 1980—and its subsequent decline—would have been less dramatic (compare the PCE index with the "PCE less food and energy index" in table 3). Inflation would have been about a point lower in 1980 and about a point higher in 1983.[9] In other words, favorable movements in food and energy prices account directly for more than two points of the decline in inflation between 1980 and 1983.

Between 1980 and 1983 the foreign exchange value of the dollar increased nearly 50 percent; this strengthening of the dollar was yet another force lowering the inflation rate. A rise in the value of the dollar lowers inflation through a number of channels, most directly through its effect on import prices. When the foreign exchange value of the dollar increases, the immediate effect is to lower the dollar price of imports in the same proportion. Although foreign producers or importers might simply take this as an opportunity to increase profit margins by raising prices (quoted in dollars) back to their old level, it is more likely that producers or importers will pass on at least some of the lower import prices to consumers in the United States. Furthermore, the effects of lower import prices are not confined to imported goods but spread through the effects of competition to domestically produced goods that are close substitutes for imports. Finally, appreciation of the dollar affects inflation through export channels. Although changes in export prices do not directly affect the prices paid by U.S. producers and consumers, a rise in the value of the dollar makes U.S. goods more expensive abroad, sometimes leading producers to cut prices and seek increased sales in the U.S. domestic market. As with imports, there may be spillover effects that lower prices of domestic goods that are close substitutes for exports.

Table 3 shows that the prices of nonoil PCE imports have indeed been volatile, aggravating inflation before 1980 and attenuating it thereafter. Comparing the "PCE less food and energy" index in table 3 with the "PCE less food, energy, and nonoil imports" index shows that favorable movements in import prices have directly reduced inflation by at least half a point. Altogether, favorable movements in food, energy, and import prices have reduced inflation by about three points compared with the amount it would have declined if these prices had increased in line with prices generally.[10]

---

9. The fixed-weight "PCE less food and energy" index rose 1.2 points less than did the fixed-weight PCE index in 1980, and 1.1 points more in 1983.

10. The inflation rate measured by the "PCE less food, energy, and imports" index declined 4.3 points between 1980 and 1983, whereas the inflation measured by the PCE index declined 7.1 points, a difference of 2.8 points. This estimate of the direct effects of food, energy, and import prices almost surely understates the impact of these volatile price changes, because it ignores any indirect or feedback effects on other prices.

Economic Slack

After taking into account measurement error and favorable movements in food, energy, and import prices, a four-point drop in consumer price inflation still remains to be explained. A simple version of the kind of equations from which Okun derived his estimate of the effect of unemployment on the inflation rate is the following:

$$p_t = p_{t-1} + a_1(U^* - U_t) + a_2(U_{t-1} - U_t)$$

where p is the inflation rate, U is the unemployment rate, U^* is the high-employment unemployment rate, and a_1 and a_2 are behavioral parameters.[11]

This equation says that this period's inflation rate will equal last period's inflation rate adjusted for the level and the rate of change in the unemployment rate. If the unemployment rate is constant at the high-employment level of about 6 percent, the inflation rate also will remain constant.[12] If unemployment is pushed below U^*, inflation will rise; and if unemployment is allowed to rise above U^*, inflation will fall. In the early stages of a recession, inflation falls both because there is economic slack and because the unemployment rate is rising. As the economy begins to recover from the recession, however, a falling unemployment rate offsets some of the downward pressure on inflation from continuing economic slack. In fact, any gains against inflation that stem from a rising unemployment rate are lost as the economy recovers and the unemployment rate falls. The size of any permanent gain against inflation depends therefore on the cumulative amount of economic slack the economy experiences.

In the equation just presented, the parameter a_1 measures this permanent change in inflation per point-year of excess unemployment, while the parameter a_2 measures the temporary gain per percentage-point increase in the unemployment rate. None of the equations examined by Okun has such a simple specification of the relationship between inflation and unemployment, but a value of 0.3 for a_1 is consistent with Okun's median estimate of the permanent gains against inflation per point-year of excess unemployment. This figure also seems to be a reasonable value for a_2.[13]

11. See Lawrence H. Summers, "The Legacy of Current Macroeconomic Policies," in Charles R. Hulten and Isabel V. Sawhill, eds., *The Legacy of Reaganomics: Prospects for Long-Term Growth* (Washington, D.C.: The Urban Institute Press, 1984).

12. This equation assumes that the unemployment rate cannot be kept below U^* without the economy's experiencing rising inflation. Not all economists accept this "accelerationist" view of the inflation process. See, for example, Robert M. Solow, "The Intelligent Citizen's Guide to Inflation," *The Public Interest*, no. 38 (Winter 1975), pp. 30–66.

13. This is the view of Summers, "The Legacy of Current Macroeconomic Policies," in Hulten and Sawhill, eds., *The Legacy of Reaganomics*. He relates inflation to the gap between actual output and potential output rather than to the unemployment gap, and his specific parameter values are somewhat more optimistic than Okun's about the output costs of lowering inflation.

According to the mainstream economists who accept this model, inflationary expectations are assumed to be formed adaptively and to change only slowly.[14] According to the rational expectations interpretation, however, expectations depend on the policy environment that exists at any particular time. In this view, past inflation has little effect on expected future inflation once a credible anti-inflationary policy has been instituted. Furthermore, past relationships between inflation and unemployment, which do not take this "credibility effect" into account, are likely to underpredict the response of inflation to a credible policy of restraint.

In the 1980–1983 period, the economy experienced ten point-years of unemployment in excess of high employment, and the unemployment rate rose nearly four points.[15] According to the mainstream equation, the high level of unemployment over this period should permanently lower the inflation rate by about three points, and the rise in the unemployment rate should produce an additional, albeit temporary, reduction in inflation of about a point. Together, these effects can account fully for the four-point decline in inflation that remains after taking into account the effects of favorable movements in food, energy, and import prices; there is no strong evidence of an additional decline in inflation arising from a rational expectations or credibility effect (table 4).[16]

---

14. In this model, the expected rate of inflation forms the basis for people's wage and price demands, but those in a particularly strong market position may be able to achieve gains in excess of these expectations while those in a weaker position will achieve smaller gains. At high employment, those experiencing above-average gains are counterbalanced by those achieving below-average gains, and the measured rate of inflation remains approximately equal to the expected rate of inflation.

If the unemployment rate drops below U^*, the number of markets with strong demand rises as does the measured inflation rate. If the excess demand persists, the expected rate of inflation will be revised upward; and even if unemployment subsequently returns to U^*, the inflation rate will be higher than it was before the episode of excess demand. If unemployment drops below U^*, the number of markets with weak demand rises and the measured inflation rate falls. If the excess supply persists, the expected rate of inflation will be revised downward; and inflation will be permanently lower once the economy returns to U^*.

15. The levels and rates of change in the unemployment rate during this period are as follows:

	U	$U - U^*$	$U_t - U_{t-1}$
1979	5.8	—	—
1980	7.1	1.1	1.3
1981	7.6	1.6	.5
1982	9.7	3.7	2.1
1983	9.6	3.6	−.1
		10.0	3.8

The 10.0 points of slack are worth 3.0 points of lower inflation (0.3 × 10.0), and the 3.8 point rise in the unemployment rate is worth 1.1 points of lower inflation (0.3 × 3.8).

16. Further evidence against a credibility effect can be found in George L. Perry, "What Have We Learned About Disinflation?" *Brookings Papers on Economic Activity*, 1983:2, pp.

TABLE 4

WHY INFLATION HAS FALLEN
(*Percentage change*)

1980 CPI inflation (December to December)	12.4	
1983 CPI inflation (December to December)	3.8	
Difference	8.6	

Causes of the Decline	Points	Percentage of Total Decline
Homeownership measurement bias[a]	1.6	18.6
Food, energy, the dollar[b]	2.9	33.7
Economic slack	4.1	47.7
High unemployment[c]	(3.0)	(34.9)
Rising unemployment[d]	(1.1)	(12.8)
Total	8.6	100

SOURCE: Authors' calculations.

a. Difference between CPI and CPI-X-1 in 1980 (table 2).

b. Difference between PCE drop of 7.1 and "PCE less food, energy, and imports" drop of 4.3, plus 0.1 for indirect effects. See text.

c. 10 point-years of unemployment between 1980 and 1983 multiplied by 0.3 points lower inflation per point-year of unemployment.

d. 3.8 point rise in unemployment multiplied by 0.3 points of lower inflation per point rise in unemployment.

How Permanent Is the Decline in Inflation?

Not all the decline in inflation between 1980 and 1983 is likely to be permanent. On average, food prices increase in line with prices generally, and, in the long run, energy prices are likely to rise somewhat faster than prices generally.[17] Thus, some of the drop in inflation due to favorable movements in food and energy prices is only temporary. Similarly, most experts consider the dollar to be overvalued by between 20 and 40 percent and expect a depreciation over the next several years. A depreciation as

---

587–602; and Otto Eckstein, "Inflation," in William Nordhaus, ed., *Inflation: Prospects and Remedies* (Washington, D.C.: Center for National Policy, 1983). Philip Cagen and William Fellner, "Tentative Lessons from the Recent Disinflationary Effort," *Brookings Papers on Economic Activity*, 1983:2, pp. 603–608, find some support for the credibility effect when looking at wage inflation. Wayne Vroman, *Wage Inflation: Prospects for Deceleration* (Washington, D.C.: The Urban Institute Press, 1983) finds a small unexplained residual in conventional wage equations.

17. The return of oil price increases in excess of the underlying inflation rate may be delayed for some time by continuing weakness in the world oil market that could forestall price increases due to rising exploration and development costs; but as the world economy recovers from the current recession, oil prices are unlikely to continue to fall as they did between 1981 and 1983.

sharp as the 1980–1983 appreciation could quickly reverse some of the gains against inflation due to appreciation. All in all, therefore, it seems reasonable to expect that about two-thirds of the three-point drop in inflation due to favorable movements in food, energy, and import prices will be lost over the next several years.

Similarly, the 1.1 point drop in inflation associated with the temporary rise in unemployment during the recession will be lost as the economy returns to high employment. But the return to high employment will not be instantaneous and the economy will experience further slack, which will act to lower inflation. According to the administration's 1985 budget forecast (January 1984), there will be an additional 5.6 point-years of excess unemployment between 1984 and the economy's return to high employment in 1988. This will lower inflation an additional 1.7 points, according to the Okun estimate.

On balance, these effects represent a one- to two-point increase in inflation, implying an inflation rate of 5 to 6 percent later in the decade.[18] Although this rate is considerably higher than the administration's estimate of 3.9 percent for 1988, it is still a considerable achievement compared with the double-digit rates of 1979 and 1980.

Economic Policy and the Decline in Inflation

These estimates show that less than half of the drop in consumer price inflation between 1980 and 1983 can be attributed directly to the economic slack experienced over this period. The rest of the decline in inflation was due to a number of favorable price movements, and at least some of this drop in inflation would have occurred irrespective of the path of macroeconomic policy.

Certainly, correcting the homeownership bias of the CPI would have lowered that measure of inflation by one to two points even if there had been no economic slack. Part of the decline in oil and commodity prices was caused by slack demand associated with a weak economy; but the conservation efforts and expansion of non-OPEC oil induced by the sharp oil price increases of the 1970s began to pay off in the 1980s, producing an oil glut and a weakening of OPEC's control of the world oil market that would have reduced oil price inflation even in a healthy world market. Otto

---

18. The precise calculation is 5.2 percent, once the economy returns to high employment. This rate assumes no movements in food, energy, or import prices beyond those discussed in the text and a smooth return to high employment in line with the Reagan administration's forecast. Obviously, unexpected price shocks or sharp deviations from the forecast recovery path would cause a different inflation rate.

Eckstein, for example, attributes only about one-third of the decline in inflation brought about by favorable oil price movements to economic slack, with these other factors accounting for the remaining two-thirds.[19]

With respect to import price inflation, the recession might have played a small role in strengthening the dollar by lowering import demand, but the sharp rise in interest rates is probably more important. That was brought about not by restrictive policies per se but by the particular mix of tight monetary policy and loose fiscal policy that prevailed after 1981.[20] With a looser monetary policy and tighter fiscal policy, interest rates would not have risen so much and the dollar would have appreciated less. Many, however, find high interest rates an inadequate explanation for the extraordinary appreciation of the dollar since 1980, arguing that some of the flow of international capital to the United States which has driven up the value of the dollar represents a growing perception by international investors that the United States is one of the few remaining "safe havens" for their savings. Thus, even without a sharp recession or high real interest rates there might have been some dollar appreciation and moderation of import price inflation, especially considering the fact that the dollar was probably somewhat undervalued in the late 1970s.

This account of the causes of the decline in inflation since 1980 indicates that the Reagan administration was mistaken in its prediction that its policies could reduce inflation without causing a severe recession. It is true that conventional models of the causes of inflation were unduly pessimistic about the decline in inflation likely to follow from restricting aggregate demand. The problem, however, was that the models failed to take into account the indirect effects of tight money and economic slack on food, oil, and import prices (and there was some additional good luck in the behavior of these prices), not that the models failed to reflect a credibility effect.[21] Conventional models of the relationship between inflation and unemployment, properly adjusted to take into account price shocks and the international repercussions of the chosen monetary and fiscal policy mix, could have fully predicted the decline in inflation achieved since 1980—if anyone had been willing to predict the depth of the recession and the height of interest rates that the administration and the Fed would have been willing to tolerate.

---

19. See Eckstein, "Inflation," in Nordhaus, ed., *Inflation: Prospects and Remedies*.

20. See chapter 2 for a discussion of the importance of the mix between monetary and fiscal policy in raising interest rates.

21. For a model that incorporates food, energy, and exchange rate effects, see Robert J. Gordon and Stephen R. King, "The Output Cost of Disinflation in Traditional and Vector Autoregressive Models," *Brookings Papers on Economic Activity*, 1982:1, pp. 205–242. Perry, "What We Have Learned About Disinflation," based his conclusion that there was no credibility effect on this model.

The Costs of the Recession

In 1979 the unemployment rate was 5.8 percent. By December 1982 it had risen to 10.7 percent, and it is not expected to return to 6 percent until 1988 according to the administration's economic projections. Although economic slack associated with unemployment rates in excess of 6 percent may have been necessary to lower inflation, the output foregone as a result of incurring this slack is a real cost that must be set against the benefits of lower inflation.

If the output that could have been produced if the unemployment rate had stayed at 6 percent is compared with the output actually produced, the disinflationary policies followed since 1979 have resulted in output losses of $654 billion (measured in constant 1982 dollars).[22] Of this total, $84 billion occurred during the 1980 recession and $570 billion occurred during the 1981–1982 recession. Furthermore, some of the costs of disinflation have not yet been paid. Even if the economy grows in line with the administration's January 1984 assumptions, an additional $316 billion of output will be lost before the economy reaches high employment in 1988 ($970 billion total loss less $654 billion loss between 1980 and 1983).[23] A more rapid growth rate of 5 percent per year would reduce the estimated losses to $217 billion, since the economy would reach high employment by 1985. A more modest growth of only 3 percent per year (perhaps associated with another recession) would impose additional costs amounting to $1.072 trillion by the time the economy returns to high employment in 1992 (see table 5).

These are large costs. They translate into billions of dollars of lost income for workers who had no job or had to accept shorter working hours or lower wages, as well as more bankruptcies and lower farm and business earnings. Most of the loss in income has been borne by workers (59 percent), with the remainder borne by corporate profits (25 percent) and farmers and individual proprietors (13 percent).[24] Adding together the income losses experienced by proprietors of unincorporated businesses and

---

22. Much of the discussion in this section is based on analysis done by Courtenay Slater and CEC Associates. They estimate that potential GNP growth slowed from 3.2 percent per year in 1979 to 2.8 percent in 1982, and that it will be 2.7 percent between 1983 and 1985, 2.4 percent between 1986 and 1990, and 2.1 percent thereafter. This slowdown is caused by demographic changes that slow the rate of growth of the labor force from 2.5 percent per year in 1979 to 1 percent per year by 1991. Meanwhile, productivity growth is assumed to increase from 1.2 percent to 1.6 percent per year.

23. Because the Reagan administration implicitly assumes stronger growth in potential output, its actual output path reaches the CEC estimate of high-employment output before the unemployment rate reaches 6 percent. Using the administration's higher potential output path would result in larger estimates of the output costs of fighting inflation.

24. The remaining 3 percent primarily represents lower indirect business taxes.

TABLE 5

LOSSES DUE TO THE 1980 AND 1981–1982 RECESSIONS,
HISTORICAL AND PROJECTED

Historical Loss	*1980*	*1981–1983*	*Total* *1980–1983*
Cumulative Loss of	(Billions of 1982 dollars)		
Gross national product[a]	84	570	654
Corporate profits	21	144	165
Profits of unincorporated businesses	11	74	85
Workers' earnings and fringe benefits by cause of loss:[b]	50	333	383
Unemployment	23	194	217
Less labor force participation	4	45	49
Reduced real wage gains	23	94	117
Earned personal income[c]	61	407	468
Less: Tax savings & transfer increases	18	131	149
Equals: Net earned personal income	43	276	319
Net earned personal income	(1982 dollars)		
Per capita	187	1,187	1,374
Per household	528	3,309	3,837
Per worker[d]	399	2,481	2,880

	Assumed Annual GNP Growth Rate Beginning in 1984 (*Year high employment is reached*)		
	3 Percent *(1992)*	*Administration* *Forecast* *(1988)*	*5 Percent* *(1985)*
Cumulative Loss of	(Billions of 1982 dollars)		
Gross national product	1,726	970	871
Net earned personal income	(1982 dollars)		
Per person	3,744	2,120	1,905
Per household	10,166	5,879	5,296
Per worker	7,694	4,413	3,973

SOURCE: CEC Associates.

NOTE: All losses are measured from the levels estimated to prevail in an economy with a 6 percent unemployment rate.

a. In addition to the losses shown for corporate profits, profits of unincorporated businesses, and workers' earnings and fringe benefits, the GNP loss includes a relatively small amount of losses of indirect business taxes, not shown separately.

b. Causes of loss of workers' earnings and fringe benefits include, in addition to those shown in the table, a small amount for fewer hours worked per week by employed workers.

c. Earned personal income consists of employee compensation (wages and fringe benefits) plus the earnings of proprietors of unincorporated businesses.

d. Per worker losses were obtained by dividing the total net loss of earned personal income by the estimated potential civilian labor force.

workers, total earned income was $468 billion lower between 1980 and 1983 as a result of economic slack. However, about one-third of this loss in the pretax earnings of individuals was offset by reduced personal income tax liabilities and increased government transfer payments; hence, disposable income for these groups fell only $319 billion. Nevertheless, the "safety net" programs that cushion income losses during a recession have replaced a smaller fraction of lost income in this recession than they did in past recessions—the direct result of the Reagan administration's cutbacks in Unemployment Insurance, Food Stamps, and other assistance programs.[25] Jobless benefits alone were about $8 billion less in 1982 than they would have been without President Reagan's policy initiatives.[26] As a result, a much lower fraction of the unemployed population received benefits than was the case in previous recessions—an estimated 45 percent during any month in 1982, for example, compared with 75 percent between 1973 and 1975.

Had the economy remained at high employment, cumulative net income per person in the United States would have been $1,374 higher between 1980 and 1983 (see table 5). The gain per household would have been about $3,837. Even if the economy recovers in line with the administration's forecast, there will be additional losses in income resulting from continuing economic slack, with the result that households will end up paying on average more than $1,000 per point of lower inflation.[27]

It is important to remember that the figures in table 5 are averages; they conceal the fact that recessions are not equal opportunity disemployers. The lower an individual's earnings and family income are to begin with, the greater the odds of being drafted into the fight against inflation. The relative income losses suffered by the working heads of poor families, for example, are four to five times as great as the losses for people heading high-income families, even after adjusting for the cushioning effect of taxes and transfers; and the 1981–1982 recession drove 4.3 million more people into poverty. At every income level, families headed by men experience greater income losses than families headed by women, and families headed by black men suffer the most of all.[28] Greater countercyclical assis-

---

25. See Courtenay Slater, "Income Loss Due to the Recession," Changing Domestic Priorities Discussion Paper (Washington, D.C.: The Urban Institute, April 1984).

26. Wayne Vroman, "The Reagan Administration and Unemployment Insurance," Changing Domestic Priorities Discussion Paper (Washington, D.C.: The Urban Institute, September 1983).

27. This is calculated on the basis of the cumulative costs shown in *table 5*, assuming the recession and continuing slack are responsible for as much as five points of the drop in inflation.

28. Edward M. Gramlich and Deborah S. Laren, "How Widespread Are Income Losses in a Recession?" in D. Lee Bawden, ed., *The Social Contract Revisited: Aims and Outcomes of President Reagan's Social Welfare Policy* (Washington, D.C.: The Urban Institute Press, 1984), table 3.

tance targeted on such groups could have ensured that the costs of fighting inflation were more evenly shared.

Summary

Substantial progress in lowering inflation was made between 1980 and 1983, but the economy paid a high price for these gains in terms of lost output and employment. The sharp drop in inflation during this period was aided by a number of favorable price movements, some of which will probably be reversed, leaving the economy with an underlying inflation rate of about 5 or 6 percent once high employment is restored. Almost all this permanent drop in inflation can be attributed to the effects of high unemployment and economic slack. The economy will end up paying about $1 trillion (measured in constant 1982 dollars) in lost output for this decline in inflation, and these costs will have been unequally distributed among the population. In the next two chapters we ask whether different policies could have avoided at least some of these costs while still making satisfactory progress against inflation.

CHAPTER 2

MONETARY AND FISCAL POLICY

The severity of the 1981–1982 recession was responsible for a substantial part of the drop in inflation between 1980 and 1983, but what accounts for the severity of the recession? In brief, actions by the Federal Reserve to lower inflation by slowing the rate of growth of the money supply turned out to be more restrictive than expected. As a result, growth in nominal income slowed abruptly from 10.8 percent in 1981 to 2.6 percent in 1982 (see the performance indicators in table 6). Had this drop in the rate of growth of nominal income been accompanied by a commensurate drop in the rate of inflation, real output could still have grown. As we have seen, however, the radical reduction in inflationary expectations required for such a result did not occur. Nearly half of the decline in the rate of growth of nominal income between 1981 and 1982 came at the expense of real output rather than inflation, and real output actually fell almost 2 percent in 1982 (see the rate of growth of real GNP in table 6).

Even though fiscal policy turned expansionary at the end of 1981 as a result of the Reagan tax cuts and defense spending increases, this fiscal stimulus was insufficient to offset the effects of monetary restraint. The initial result of this clash between fiscal expansion and monetary restraint was a rise in interest rates and a strengthening of the dollar. It was not until monetary policy became less restrictive in late 1982 that the economy began to recover from the recession. Fiscal policy had by this time become expansionary as well, and the borrowing needs of the Treasury kept real interest rates high and the dollar strong.

In this chapter we analyze these monetary and fiscal policy developments. In the next, we explore the question of whether different policies could have avoided, or at least moderated the recession and, if so, how much less inflation would have come down.

27

TABLE 6

Economic Policy and Performance Indicators, 1971–1983

	1971	1972	1973	1974	1975	1976	1977	1978	1979	1980	1981	1982	1983
Monetary Policy Indicators													
Rate of growth of M1	6.7	8.5	5.8	4.8	5.0	6.1	8.2	8.2	7.4	7.2	5.1	8.5	9.6
Rate of growth of real M1	2.0	4.0	−1.2	−4.9	−2.5	1.4	1.9	−0.3	−0.7	−2.7	−3.3	3.9	5.3
Rate of growth of M1 velocity	2.7	2.8	5.5	2.2	4.8	3.0	3.7	6.0	2.1	2.0	5.4	−5.5	0.2
Federal funds rate	4.7	4.4	8.7	10.5	5.8	5.0	5.5	7.9	11.2	13.4	16.4	12.3	9.1
Real federal funds rate[a]	0.0	0.2	1.6	0.3	−1.9	0.4	−0.6	−0.5	3.0	3.2	7.7	7.9	5.0
Fiscal Policy Indicators (as a percentage of GNP)													
Federal expenditures[b]	20.5	20.6	19.9	20.9	23.0	22.4	22.0	21.3	21.1	22.9	23.3	24.9	25.0
Federal receipts[b]	18.4	19.2	19.5	20.1	18.5	19.3	19.6	19.9	20.4	20.6	21.2	10.1	19.4
Federal budget deficit(−)[b]	−2.0	−1.4	−0.4	−0.8	−4.5	−3.1	−2.4	−1.4	−0.7	−2.3	−2.1	−4.8	−5.5
High-employment deficit(−) or surplus[c]	−1.1	−1.0	−0.7	0.0	−1.8	−1.0	−1.1	−0.7	−0.1	−0.7	0.2	−1.0	−1.8
Debt held by public	29.5	28.7	27.4	25.1	26.8	29.3	29.6	29.2	27.3	27.8	27.6	30.4	35.4
Real high-employment deficit(−) or surplus[d]	1.2	1.5	1.5	1.1	0.6	0.7	−1.3	1.3	1.9	1.3	1.7	0.5	−0.9
Change in high-employment budget	−0.6	0.1	0.3	0.7	−1.8	0.8	−0.1	0.4	0.6	−0.6	0.9	−1.2	−0.8
Change in real deficit	−0.2	0.2	0.1	−0.4	−0.5	0.1	0.6	0.2	0.4	−0.6	0.5	−1.3	−1.3
Performance Indicators													
Rate of growth of GNP	9.6	11.5	11.6	7.1	10.0	9.3	12.2	14.7	9.7	9.3	10.8	2.6	10.4
Rate of growth of real GNP	4.7	7.0	4.2	−2.8	2.2	4.4	5.7	5.8	1.4	−0.8	2.0	−1.7	6.1
Inflation rate (GNP deflator)	4.7	4.3	7.1	10.2	7.7	4.7	6.1	8.5	8.2	10.2	8.7	4.4	4.1
Unemployment rate (civilian)	5.9	5.6	4.9	5.6	8.5	7.7	7.1	6.1	5.8	7.1	7.6	9.7	9.6

Sources: Federal Reserve Board, BEA, BLS, Office of Management and Budget.

Note: All growth rates are fourth-quarter-to-fourth-quarter percentage changes.

a. Federal funds rate less rate of growth of GNP deflator.

b. National Income and Products Account basis.

c. Based on 6 percent unemployment.

d. Change in debt held by the public as a share of GNP less the difference between actual and high-employment deficits as a share of GNP.

Monetary Policy

Monetary policy is the responsibility of the independent Federal Reserve Board. An understanding of monetary policy developments in the Reagan years requires some understanding of the channels through which Fed actions affect economic activity.

The Fed, the Money Supply, and the Economy

In its role as central banker, the Fed establishes the conditions under which banks accept deposits and hold reserves against those deposits. By buying and selling government bonds, in what are called open market operations, or, less frequently, by changing reserve requirements or the conditions under which banks can borrow reserves at its discount window, the Fed expands or contracts the supply of reserves, strongly influencing interest rates, the money supply, and ultimately output, employment, and inflation.

The Fed, however, does not have full control over the money supply, much less the level of economic activity. Unless the links between Fed actions that affect bank reserves and the subsequent response of the banking system in expanding or contracting the supply of money and credit are rigid, the Fed will not be able to control the money supply precisely.[1] Even if the Fed were able to control the money supply with a high degree of precision, it would not be able to control economic activity precisely unless the links between changes in the supply of money and credit and subsequent changes in economic activity are also quite stable.

Among economists, there is considerable disagreement about how closely the monetary instruments that the Fed can control are linked to the broad macroeconomic policy variables that are the real concern of monetary policy. As a result, there is also considerable disagreement about how the Fed should conduct monetary policy.

Monetarists believe that controlling the rate of growth of the money supply is the key to controlling economic activity and that it is an error to allow the money supply to grow erratically in an attempt to influence the behavior of interest rates. Many believe further (1) that the Fed should

---

1. Banks are required to hold a fraction of their deposits as reserves, but they may choose to hold excess reserves or they may be able to borrow reserves from the Fed in order to support more deposits than their own reserves allow. The multiplier between reserves and the money supply varies with changes in the ratio of excess or borrowed reserves to required reserves and with changes in the composition of deposits (since different kinds of deposits have different reserve requirements). Unless the Fed is able to anticipate and offset changes in bank behavior that affect these variables, there will be some looseness in the link between reserves and the money supply.

strive for a constant rate of growth in the money supply consistent with the long-term real growth of the economy; (2) that such a strategy would be feasible if the proper operating procedures were in place;[2] and (3) that such steady monetary growth would produce greater price stability and steadier real growth than would be the case if the Fed were to try to "fine tune" economic activity by changing the rate of growth of the money supply in response to short-term fluctuations in interest rates, unemployment, output, or inflation.

Nonmonetarists disagree. They believe, first, that the links between changes in bank reserves and subsequent changes in the money supply are so variable and unpredictable that no set of operating procedures can guarantee that the close control of the money supply favored by monetarists is attainable in the short run.[3] More important, they question the desirability of keeping the money supply on a predetermined growth path in the absence of a stable relationship between money and economic activity. They argue that the ratio of GNP to the money supply, the so called "velocity" of money, shows sufficient variability that the failure to adjust the money supply in response to changes in velocity will impart needless instability to the growth path of nominal income.[4]

---

2. The Fed's operating procedures include such things as the method by which banks are to calculate their required reserves, the terms under which banks can borrow at the Fed's discount window, and the specific financial variable to be used as the instrument for controlling money. Monetarists argue that the Fed would have been able to control the money supply more closely in the past if it had used contemporaneous reserve accounting rather than the lagged reserve accounting actually in place between 1968 and 1983 and if it had employed the monetary base (total reserves plus currency in circulation) rather than interest rates or nonborrowed reserves as its instrument. See, for example, Milton Friedman, "Lessons from the 1979-82 Monetary Policy Experiment," *The American Economic Review*, May 1984, pp. 397-400.

3. See Ralph C. Bryant, *Controlling Money* (Washington, D.C.: The Brookings Institution, 1983), chapter 4. Bryant acknowledges that the operating procedures favored by monetarists give the Fed greater control over the money supply than other operating procedures in the face of unexpected fluctuations in aggregate demand. But he points out that other operating procedures work better in the face of other kinds of nonpolicy disturbances, including unexpected shifts in the demand for currency or demand deposits, unexpected changes in banks' willingness to hold excess reserves, and unexpected changes in discount-window borrowing. Furthermore, Bryant argues, nonpolicy disturbances that deflect the money supply from any predetermined target path are likely to occur under any set of operating procedures.

4. Monetary theory suggests that people will hold smaller cash balances when interest rates are high than when they are low, hence velocity is likely to rise when interest rates rise. Also, if people expect the income losses in a recession to be temporary, they may not reduce their money demand in proportion to their income loss, causing velocity to fall during recessions and rise during recoveries. Besides these systematic variations in velocity, there may be unexpected shifts in people's preference for holding money versus other assets that cause unpredictable shifts in velocity. See Congressional Budget Office, *The Economic and Budget Outlook: An Update* (Washington, D.C.: Government Printing Office, September 1982), pp. 79-85.

Was There a Monetarist Experiment?

In stating its goals for monetary policy, the Reagan administration placed itself squarely in the monetarist camp.[5] It called for a gradual, steady reduction in the rate of growth of money and credit to levels consistent with the noninflationary expansion of the economy. Moreover, the Reagan administration expressed the monetarist beliefs (1) that variability in the rate of growth of the money supply resulting from past efforts at fine tuning had played an important role in producing the disappointing economic performance of the 1970s; (2) that past Fed concern with interest rates had been inappropriate; and (3) that steady, predictable growth in the money supply was critical for achieving sustained, noninflationary growth.

The Fed had never embraced monetarism to this degree, but in its efforts to control inflation during the 1970s, it had begun to turn away from an earlier concern with the behavior of interest rates and to pay increasing attention to the behavior of the money supply. In the mid-1970s the Fed began to set targets for the rates of growth of the major money and credit aggregates it sought to control.[6] With the passage of the Humphrey-Hawkins Act in 1978, the Fed began to submit formal reports to Congress that included its money and credit targets. Nevertheless, the money supply often grew faster than the Fed wanted, and in October 1979 it announced a change in its operating procedures aimed at improving its ability to meet its targets for slowing the rate of growth of money and credit. Although this change was essentially technical,[7] it came at a time when the Fed was

---

5. See *America's New Beginning. A Program for Economic Recovery*, Part 1, pp. 22-23.

6. The Fed currently sets target growth rates for three monetary aggregates and one credit aggregate as follows:

M1 is the most narrowly defined monetary aggregate and is meant to include those assets—but only those assets—that serve as media of exchange and thus meet the transactions demand for money. M1 currently comprises currency, demand deposits at commercial banks, other checkable deposits (primarily NOW accounts and automatic-transfer savings accounts), and travelers' checks.

M2 is a broader measure that encompasses the role of money as a store of value as well as a medium of exchange. It adds to M1 other highly liquid assets which are readily available for transactions but which are judged to be held primarily for portfolio purposes.

M3 is a still broader measure that includes other highly liquid assets of more limited use in transactions because of their size or conventions concerning their use.

Total debt of domestic nonfinancial sectors is the credit aggregate used by the Fed. It comprises borrowing by private, domestic, nonfinancial sectors and by the federal, state, and local governments in United States markets and from abroad. It excludes borrowing by foreigners in the United States.

7. The Fed abandoned a strategy that used interest rates as its instrument for controlling money and credit and adopted a strategy that used the supply of reserves.

Before this change was made, the Fed had tried to estimate the federal funds rate (the rate determined in the interbank market for reserves) that would elicit the demand for money

eager to reassure jittery financial markets of its commitment to slowing the rate of growth in the money supply in order to lower inflation.

With these changes, the Fed seemed to move closer to a monetarist approach; yet there is no evidence of either a declining growth trend or greater steadiness in the actual behavior of the money supply after 1979. Figure 4 shows that the rate of growth in the money supply has continued to be high relative to the rate of growth in real output and highly volatile. In fact, the money supply (M1) grew faster in 1983 than it did in 1980, and its average rate of growth during the Reagan years has been as high as the rate during the Carter years (table 6).

Figure 5 shows the behavior of the principal aggregates, M1 and M2, relative to their annual target ranges. Two things are noteworthy. First, the Fed has not gradually and steadily lowered its targets: the target ranges for both M1 and M2 were higher in 1983 than they were in 1980. In fact, in the summer of 1982, the Fed suspended its targets for M1 and allowed M1 to rise well above its original upper limit; in the summer of 1983 the Fed explicitly raised and widened its target range for M1. Second, M1 has sometimes risen above and sometimes fallen below its target range, while M2 was consistently at the top of its range until the second half of 1983. As a result, the behavior of the two aggregates with respect to their target ranges has sometimes diverged significantly. In the second half of 1981, for example, when M1 plunged below its target range, M2 remained above its target range. Although traditionally the Fed had focused on M1 as its principal policy target, in 1983 the Fed began to pay more attention to M2.

There is thus little evidence in the Fed's setting of monetary targets or in the actual behavior of the money supply that the Fed was pursuing the administration's stated monetarist objective of gradually and steadily reducing the rate of growth in the money supply. Given the relatively rapid rates of growth in the money supply in recent years, it does not even appear that the Fed was supporting the administration's broader objective of lowering inflation, but this conclusion would be wrong. Although the rate of

---

and credit it wished to supply and it had conducted open market operations so as to keep the federal funds rate within a narrow range around this target value. Such a strategy required, however, that the Fed fully accommodate unexpected fluctuations in the demand for money and credit. Because the Fed frequently underestimated the funds rate necessary to achieve its money growth targets, the money supply grew more rapidly than was intended.

With the adoption of a reserves strategy, the Fed began to try to estimate the quantity of reserves that would induce the banking system to supply the amount of money and credit the Fed wished to see made available. Under this approach, unexpected fluctuations in the demand for money and credit are not fully accommodated since interest rates rise to choke off some of the increase in the demand for money. Thus, somewhat closer control of the money supply is possible.

For a monetarist argument that the Fed's operating procedures remained inadequate, see Friedman, "Lessons from the 1979–82 Monetary Policy Experiments."

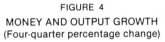

FIGURE 4
MONEY AND OUTPUT GROWTH
(Four-quarter percentage change)

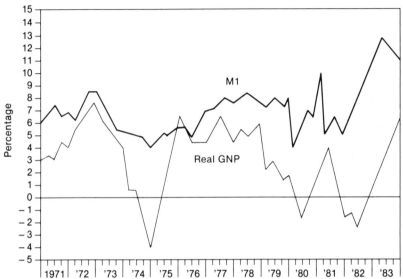

SOURCES: The Federal Reserve Board, "Money Stock Revisions" (mimeographed),
March 1984, table 1; and the BEA.

growth in the money supply is the indicator that receives the most attention, it is not always the best indicator of the direction of monetary policy.
This was especially true between 1979 and 1983.

For one thing, the rate of growth in the nominal money supply does
not reflect the effect of inflation in eroding the real value of money. Even
though the rate of growth in the money supply may be high in a period of
inflation, the supply of money and credit to finance real spending will actually fall unless the rate of growth in the money supply exceeds the inflation
rate. Table 6 shows, for example, that after rising in 1976 and 1977, the
real money supply fell between 1978 and 1981 before rising sharply once
again in 1982 and 1983.

Even changes in the real money supply are an inadequate measure of
the thrust of monetary policy if the demand for money is changing at the
same time. Suppose, for example, people wish to hold more cash balances

FIGURE 5

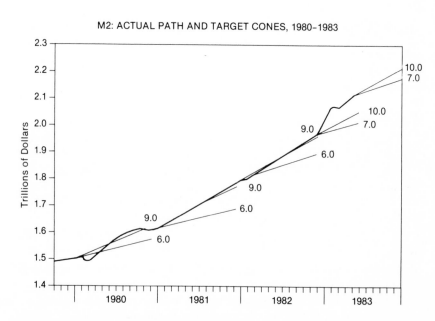

M1: ACTUAL PATH AND TARGET CONES, 1980-1983

M2: ACTUAL PATH AND TARGET CONES, 1980-1983

SOURCE: Board of Governors of the Federal Reserve System.

at any level of income. Unless the money supply expands in line with this increase in money demand, there will be less money available to finance spending. Figure 6 shows that velocity has varied considerably over the years, indicating that the quantity of money demanded as a proportion of income has indeed varied over time. The behavior of velocity in 1982 is particularly noteworthy. The rise in the demand for money relative to income was so strong that velocity fell 5.5 percent, more than offsetting a 3.9 percent increase in the real money supply. In 1983 the real money supply grew rapidly, but so did the demand for money; hence the stimulus to spending was less than would have been the case if velocity had grown as well.

The final indicator of the direction of monetary policy reported in table 6 is the interbank lending rate (the federal funds rate). A rise in the real federal funds rate indicates either an explicit tightening by the Fed or at least a resistance by the Fed to accommodating a rise in money demand. A fall in the real federal funds rate indicates either an explicit easing in the money supply or a decline in the demand for money that is not offset by an equivalent decline in supply. A high real federal funds rate indicates relatively tight money, whereas a low federal funds rate indicates relatively easy money. The real federal funds rate was quite low during most of the 1970s, but rose sharply between 1979 and 1982. Despite some easing in 1983 it remains very high, indicating continued restraint by the Fed.

Many nonmonetarists view the Fed's continuing to exercise monetary restraint well into a severe recession as evidence that its strategy was essentially monetarist, no matter what the actual behavior of the money supply. According to monetarists, however, the continued variability in the rate of growth of the money supply after 1979 is evidence that the Fed never truly adopted monetarism. Certainly, when the Fed suspended its targets for M1 in the summer of 1982 and announced in October that it would henceforth consider a variety of indicators, including interest rates, in setting policy, it explicitly abandoned monetarist principles. Nevertheless, the Fed does seem to have followed a sustained policy of monetary restraint during this period, and the close attention paid to the behavior of the money supply between October 1979 and October 1982 may be the closest we will ever come in the real world to a monetarist experiment.

Monetary Policy and Economic Performance: 1979–1983

Monetarists and nonmonetarists alike have been critical of the Fed's performance since 1979—but from very different perspectives. Monetarists argue that the continuing volatility of income and output since 1979 has been aggravated by the Fed's failure to keep the money supply growing at a constant rate, whereas nonmonetarists argue that the volatility has

FIGURE 6

PERCENTAGE CHANGE IN VELOCITY OF M1, 1971–1983
(Four-quarter percentage change)

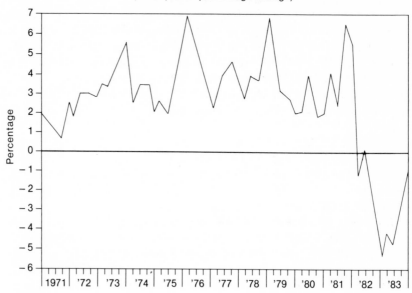

PERCENTAGE CHANGE IN VELOCITY OF M2, 1971–1983
(Four-quarter percentage change)

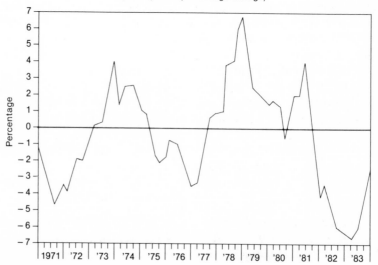

SOURCE: Board of Governors of the Federal Reserve System.

been aggravated by the Fed's sticking to its targets too long in the face of an unprecedented drop in the velocity of money.

The monetarists' case for keeping the rate of growth in the money supply constant emerged during a period in which, they argue, Fed attempts to stabilize interest rates rather than the money supply resulted in its too readily accommodating expansionary aggregate demand shocks, including excessive fiscal stimulus.[8] A policy aimed at keeping the money supply growing at a predetermined rate would have produced greater stability in income because unanticipated surges in aggregate demand would have been partially damped by rising interest rates.

In principle, however, there are times when it is better to stabilize interest rates than to stabilize the rate of growth of the money supply, assuming the real goal of monetary policy is to stabilize fluctuations in income around its long-run noninflationary growth path.[9] Suppose, for example, there is an unexpected increase in the demand for money unrelated to changes in aggregate demand or interest rates. A policy of keeping the money stock on a predetermined growth path will result in an unexpected and undesirable reduction in national income, because the rise in money demand will not be accommodated by a rise in the money supply. In contrast, a policy aimed at keeping interest rates within a predetermined range would appropriately allow the money supply to rise and accommodate the unexpected increase in money demand, allowing income to remain on its predetermined path.

Although the economy may have been prone primarily to demand shocks in the late 1960s and early 1970s, when the Fed first began to move toward a monetarist approach, the years since 1973 have seen greater instability in the supply side of the real economy and in the money and credit markets. These make the case for a money growth rule less appealing than it once may have been.[10] Furthermore, financial innovation—the development of new kinds of accounts, new banking services, and new financial institutions, especially since the substantial deregulation of banking that began in 1980—has altered traditional relationships between money and economic activity. We are still in the process of determining how to define and measure money and relate such new measures to economic activity.[11]

---

8. See the discussion about the rise of inflation in the late 1960s and early 1970s in chapter 1.

9. See William Poole, "Optimal Choice of Monetary Policy Instruments in a Simple Stochastic Macro Model," *Quarterly Journal of Economics*, vol. 84 (May 1970), pp. 197–216.

10. See, for example, Benjamin M. Friedman, "Time to Assess the Monetary Targets Framework," Harvard Discussion Paper Number 875, processed, January 1982, p. 5.

11. One example of this difficulty has been the Fed's effort to adjust for the effects of financial deregulation and the shift of money into NOW accounts. The part of NOW account balances that satisfies a transactions motive should properly be included in M1, but the part

The result of all this uncertainty is that the stability and the predictability of the relationship between money and economic activity that are so important for the success of a money growth strategy, have been absent. Since the economy continues to be subject to aggregate demand shocks, an interest rate strategy is not a clearly superior alternative. In principle, a policy of flexible accommodation to different economic circumstances with a focus on a variety of economic indicators, but particularly national income, seems preferable to strict adherence to either an interest rate strategy or a money growth rule. However, the possibility exists—and it is emphasized by monetarists—that the Fed will more often than not be unable to discern, or will misinterpret, changes in market conditions and will take inappropriate actions that actually aggravate the effects of the unpredictable shocks that will inevitably occur.

Although this may have happened in the past, it does not seem to have been the case since 1979. The data in table 7 suggest that the Fed has generally responded in the right direction to surprises in the relationship between money and economic activity. This can be seen by comparing the actual behavior of the money supply and velocity with the Fed's money growth targets and its implicit projections for velocity growth.[12]

Historically, M1 velocity has grown at about 3 percent per year as financial innovation has allowed households and firms to economize on their transactions balances, while M2 velocity has shown no trend. At first, the Fed seems to have set targets for money growth aimed at slowing nominal income growth based on velocity's increasing within its historical range (table 7). When velocity turned out to be highly unstable, however, the Fed often adjusted to this variability in the right direction to offset some of the variability. In 1980, for example, velocity grew slowly and the Fed allowed money growth to exceed its target (although variability over the year in the rate of money growth was high). Even so, the real money supply fell 2.7

---

that satisfies a savings motive should not be. In the years since 1979 the Fed has experimented with different definitions of the money supply and with ad hoc "shift" adjustments in characterizing its monetary targets in an effort to maintain an M1 measure that corresponds to the old transactions balance concept. Since there is uncertainty about how to do this, some of the observed volatility of velocity during this period may be more indicative of the difficulty of defining money than of fundamental volatility in the demand for money.

12. Within the Fed, the course of monetary policy is set by the Federal Open Market Committee (FOMC), which meets in secret about every six weeks. Although the minutes of FOMC meetings are eventually released—and they indicate Fed goals with respect to intermediate targets like the money supply or interest rates—they say little about the ultimate goals of policy with respect to income, output, inflation, or unemployment that motivate the setting of these intermediate targets. The FOMC does report summary data on members' individual forecasts for these variables and these, together with the Fed's targets for money growth, form the basis for the projections reported in table 7.

TABLE 7

MONETARY POLICY, 1980–1984

(Percentage change, fourth quarter to fourth quarter)

| | 1980 | | 1981 | | 1982 | | 1983 | | 1984 |
	Actual	*Projected*[a]	*Actual*	*Projected*[a]	*Actual*	*Projected*[a]	*Actual*	*Projected*[a]	*Projected*[a]
Nominal GNP	9.3	8.5–11.5	10.8	8.5–11.5	2.6	9.5–12.3	10.4	7.0– 9.5	7.0–10.3
Real GNP	−0.8	−0.5– 2.0	2.0	0.5– 3.0	−1.7	1.0– 4.0	6.1	2.5– 4.0	3.0– 5.0
GNP deflator	10.2	8.5–10.5	8.7	7.8– 9.5	4.4	6.5– 8.5	4.1	4.0– 5.8	3.7– 6.5
M1	7.2	4.0– 6.5	5.1	6.0– 8.5	8.5	2.5– 5.5	9.6	4.0– 8.0	4.0– 8.0
M1 velocity	2.0	4.5	5.4	2.6	−5.5	6.6	0.2	2.1	2.5
M2	9.0	6.0– 9.0	9.6	6.0– 9.0	9.4	6.0– 9.0	11.8	7.0–10.0	6.5– 9.5
M2 velocity	0.3	2.3	1.3	2.3	−6.2	3.1	−1.3	−0.2	0.6

SOURCES: U.S. Department of Commerce, BEA; and Board of Governors of the Federal Reserve System.

a. Federal Open Market Committee member projections contained in monetary public report to Congress in July of previous year. Projections for growth in M1 and M2 velocity calculated from midpoints of nominal GNP projections and money targets.

percent (table 6) and the economy experienced a brief recession.[13] In 1981 velocity grew more rapidly, but the Fed offset this incipient stimulus by holding the rate of growth of the money supply below its target. The real money supply fell another 3.3 percent.

In 1982, velocity declined sharply, causing nominal GNP to be much lower than it would have been if velocity had remained within its expected range. Even strong growth in the real money supply was not enough to offset the contractionary effects of this unexpected drop in velocity. The recession was thus worse than it would have been if velocity had not fallen so sharply. The volatile behavior of velocity, along with other factors, such as the mounting international debt crisis, is what led the Fed to suspend its money targets and allow M1 to grow rapidly through the first half of 1983. By the end of 1983, however, as velocity was returning to more normal rates of growth, the Fed began to slow the rate of growth of the money supply as well (figure 7).

Suppose the Fed had not tried to offset shifts in velocity but had instead pursued the Reagan economic recovery program prescription and steadily reduced the rate of growth in the money supply.[14] Figure 7 shows that such a policy would have produced even greater volatility in income growth than the policies actually followed (assuming velocity had followed the same erratic path it actually did follow over this period). Unless one thinks that most of the volatility in the rate of growth of velocity would have been absent if a different path of money growth had been followed, the Fed's willingness to deviate from its predetermined monetary targets did not compromise the broader policy objectives of the Reagan administration.

Both the Fed and the administration placed paramount importance on reducing inflation. The Fed did not pursue a purely monetarist strategy for achieving this objective, but neither did it back off and allow an inflationary expansion of the economy at the first sign of rising unemployment. In this sense, then, the Fed provided the administration with the monetary policy it sought. The administration's willingness to tolerate a rise in unemployment may, in turn, have strengthened the Fed's resolve. An administration less tolerant of high unemployment would have brought pressure to bear on the Fed to loosen monetary policy sooner than it did, but it is a moot question whether the Fed would have bowed to such pressure and altered course significantly.

13. The short, sharp 1980 recession was brought on when the Carter administration, worried about rapidly rising inflation at the beginning of the year, urged the Fed to initiate a policy of severe credit restraint. When these restraints were later lifted, the economy began to recover.

14. The administration based its original economic forecast on the assumption that the growth rates of money and credit would be steadily reduced to half their 1980 levels by 1986. For M1, this implies a reduction from 7.2 percent per year to 3.6 percent per year. See *America's New Beginning*, p. 23.

FIGURE 7

THE PATH OF GNP
UNDER DIFFERENT MONETARY POLICIES, 1981-1983

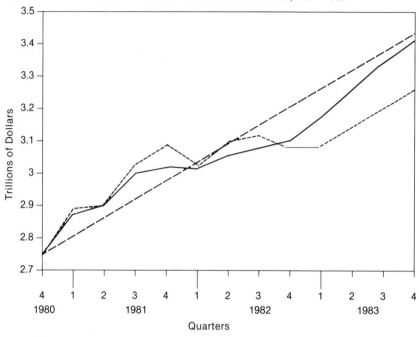

Actual GNP
GNP with Reagan administration monetary policy and actual velocity
GNP with Reagan administration monetary policy and constant velocity

SOURCES: BEA and authors' simulations

NOTES: GNP with Reagan monetary policies and actual velocity calculated by applying actual velocity each quarter to a money supply path that lowers M1
growth from 7.2 percent per year in 1980 to 3.6 percent per year in 1986.
GNP with Reagan monetary policies and constant velocity assumes GNP
growth falls smoothly to half its 1980 rate by 1986.

The Role of Fiscal Policy

The Reagan administration argued that rising taxes and government
expenditures and large budget deficits were as important as excessive
growth in the money supply in causing the poor economic performance of
the 1970s. The Reagan administration's economic recovery program called
for a reduction in federal outlays and receipts from their 1980 levels to less

than 20 percent of GNP by 1986 and a balanced budget by 1984.[15] At the same time, however, the administration sought a substantial increase in spending for national defense. Figure 8 shows that taxes and expenditures did grow somewhat as a share of GNP during the 1970s and that there were persistent budget deficits. But the figure also shows that, although taxes did indeed fall as a share of GNP after 1980, expenditures actually increased and the budget deficit has grown rather than shrunk.[16]

There has indeed been a sharp change in the direction of fiscal policy under President Reagan, but except for the tax cuts, it has not been the change the administration originally sought. The president's original budget forecast was based on highly optimistic economic assumptions and included budget savings that had not yet been specified. The budget bill enacted by Congress in the summer of 1981[17] included substantial cuts, but not all that the president requested and certainly not enough to meet the administration's outlay objectives. Congress has subsequently proved reluctant to make further substantial cuts in spending.

Poor economic performance together with the substantial tax cuts enacted in the summer of 1981[18] reduced revenues and produced large budget deficits. Passage of tax increases in 1982, 1983, and 1984[19] undid some of the cuts of 1981 but not enough to eliminate the prospect of large budget deficits for the indefinite future. Faced with the need to make choices among conflicting budget objectives and a Congress that was unwilling to make further substantial nondefense spending cuts, the administration was more willing to accept large deficits than to raise taxes or cut defense spending.

---

15. See *America's New Beginning*, Part I, pp. 1-15, Part II, p. 7.

16. The budget concept used here is the National Income and Product Accounts (NIA) budget, which differs from the unified budget concept used in the president's budget. Although the latter concept is more appropriate for some purposes, the NIA budget is better for analyzing aggregate economic activity because it measures the federal government's contribution to current income and output. The two budget concepts differ somewhat in their geographical coverage and treatment of the timing of some receipts and expenditures. Also, they treat the netting and grossing of some items differently, most notably federal government contributions to employee retirement, which are netted out in the unified budget but which appear in both receipts and expenditures in the NIA budget. Note, however, that netting and grossing considerations do not affect comparisons of the deficits under different budget concepts. Finally, the NIA budget excludes federal loans and receipts from offshore oil leases, because they are transfers and do not contribute to current income and output.

17. The Omnibus Budget Reconciliation Act of 1981.

18. The Economic Recovery Tax Act (ERTA).

19. The Tax Equity and Fiscal Responsibility Act (TEFRA), which, among other things, repealed some of the business tax cuts of 1981, was enacted in 1982; gasoline taxes were raised in 1982; payroll taxes were increased in 1983; and a number of "loopholes" were closed as part of the Deficit Reduction Act of 1984.

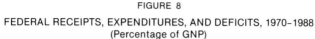

FIGURE 8

FEDERAL RECEIPTS, EXPENDITURES, AND DEFICITS, 1970–1988
(Percentage of GNP)

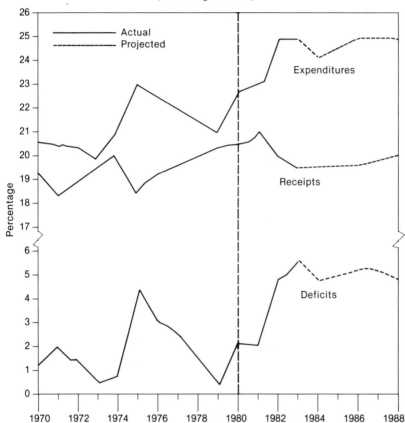

SOURCES: BEA for actual figures; authors' simulations using the DRI model for projections.

Measuring the Reagan Administration's Budget Deficits

To put the Reagan administration's budget deficits in perspective, the
first column of table 8 shows the average budget deficit as a percentage of
GNP for selected electoral periods from 1953 through 1988. These data
show quite clearly that the Reagan administration's budget deficits, aver-

TABLE 8

Federal Budget Deficits and Debt
(*Percentage of GNP*)

	Deficit[a]		
Periods	*Actual*	*High Employment*	*Debt[b]*
1953–1960	−0.3	0.7	53.4
1961–1964	−0.5	0.8	44.5
1965–1968	−0.6	−1.0	36.4
1969–1972	−1.0	−0.3	29.6
1973–1976	−2.2	−0.9	27.2
1977–1980	−1.7	−0.7	28.5
1981–1984	−4.3	−1.4	32.7
1985–1988	−5.2	−2.8	40.1

a. Both the actual and the high-employment deficit are calculated on a National Income and Products Account (NIA) basis for calendar years. Sources: *Survey of Current Business*, various issues, for historical data; authors' simulations using the DRI model for projections, assuming the policies in effect as of March 1984 will be continued.

b. The debt/GNP ratio is debt held by the public divided by GNP for fiscal years. Source: *Budget of the United States Government, FY 1985, Special Analyses*, Special Analysis E (Washington, D.C.: Government Printing Office, 1984), Table E-3.

aging 4.3 percent of GNP between 1981 and 1984, and the prospect of deficits averaging 5.2 percent of GNP between 1985 and 1988, are without precedent over this period.

It is now widely recognized that changes in the actual budget deficit are a poor measure of changes in the thrust of fiscal policy, because the budget is sensitive to the level of economic activity as well as to policy changes. To isolate the effect of policy changes, it is customary to measure the budget deficit at a standardized level of economic activity: the larger the standardized deficit, other things being equal, the greater the stimulus to spending from fiscal policy.

During the 1970s, the budget deficit standardized at a 6 percent un-employment rate (the high-employment budget) was, on average, less than 1 percent of GNP (tables 6 and 8).[20] Higher deficits resulted when temporary countercyclical fiscal stimulus was applied during recessions, but the trend during this period was, if anything, downward. Beginning in 1982, however, the high-employment budget deficit began to rise, and it is projected to average nearly 3 percent of GNP for the rest of the decade (table 8).

20. Standardizing at a different level of economic activity would change the size of the standardized budget deficit, but it would have much less effect on the size of *changes* in that deficit.

Recently, some economists have come to believe that the high-employment budget deficit should be adjusted for the erosion of outstanding government debt due to inflation.[21] Corrected for the new debt needed to finance the cyclical component of the budget deficit, the change in the ratio of debt to GNP provides a rough-and-ready measure of this "real" high-employment deficit. Rising inflation in the late 1970s caused such a large erosion of the real value of the debt that this measure actually showed a surplus from 1976 to 1979 (table 6). The real high-employment deficit tends to change in line with the unadjusted high-employment deficit, although the levels for the two deficits are different. Thus, the increase in the high-employment deficit after 1982 was mirrored in the change from surplus to deficit in the real high-employment deficit and the rise in the ratio of debt to GNP (table 8).

Short-Run Effects of Rising Deficits

Such a dramatic change in fiscal policy can be expected to have two effects on the economy. On the one hand, aggregate demand for goods and services will be stimulated by increases in government purchases and by tax cuts that encourage more consumption and investment. On the other hand, investment, purchases of consumer durables, and net exports will be discouraged by rising interest rates unless monetary policy is accommodative. Although when the Reagan administration's budget deficits first emerged there was much talk that this latter effect could be so strong as to dominate the former and prevent the economy's recovery from the 1981–1982 recession, there was never much theoretical support for such a view. The recovery from the 1981–1982 recession has, in fact, been quite strong, despite the presence of large budget deficits and high interest rates.[22]

---

21. Such an adjustment would put government accounting practices more in line with private accounting practices. Large declines in the real value of outstanding government debt during the 1970s reduced the real value of outstanding liabilities and produced a steady improvement in the federal government's real balance sheet, despite persistent budget deficits. This improvement in federal government net worth was, of course, exactly offset by a decline in private sector net worth. By ignoring this source of restraint, the current budget deficit overstates the amount of spending stimulus from fiscal policy. See Robert Eisner and Paul J. Pieper, "A New View of the Federal Debt and Budget Deficits," *The American Economic Review*, vol. 74, no. 1 (March 1984), pp. 11–29.

22. Fiscal stimulus raises the demand for goods and services at any given interest rate. Unless monetary policy is completely accommodative, however, interest rates will rise and partially offset some of this stimulus. Unless the demand for money is completely insensitive to interest rates or monetary policy is conducted so as to maintain a given level of income, some increase in output and some increase in interest rates will be associated with fiscal stimulus. The argument that the effect of higher interest rates is stronger than the effect of greater demand confuses a rise in interest rates *caused by* greater demand with a rise in interest rates

Still, the strength of the recovery tells us nothing about the effect of the Reagan administration's fiscal policy, compared with an alternative policy that would have been less expansionary. To compare actual policy with a hypothetical alternative requires the use of a model showing how changes in fiscal policy affect the economy. We have chosen to use the Data Resources, Inc. (DRI), quarterly model of the U.S. economy, a large-scale econometric forecasting model whose structure generally reflects conventional macroeconomic theory. Numerous objections, both practical and conceptual, have arisen with respect to the reliability of such models, both in forecasting and in simulating policy changes, but as yet there is no satisfactory alternative for assessing quantitative magnitudes. Any results must be tempered with a healthy dose of skepticism, but judicious use and interpretation of the model's results can provide some helpful insights into the quantitative importance of the fiscal stimulus provided by the Reagan administration's budget and tax program.[23]

As an alternative to the Reagan administration's fiscal policy, we looked at a policy that keeps the standardized budget deficit approximately in balance. We assumed that Congress and any administration would have been sensitive to the effect of bracket creep in raising the share of taxes in GNP. Therefore, we assumed that personal income taxes were indexed for inflation beginning in fiscal year 1982. We assumed no business tax cut, but we note that to the extent that rising inflation artificially raised the business tax base during the 1970s, any subsequent decline in inflation would be equivalent to a business tax cut. We assumed further that Congress and any administration would have wished to continue the increase in real defense spending begun during the Carter administration. Therefore, we assumed a substantial, but more modest, increase in real defense spending. Finally, we assumed that growth in nondefense expenditures would have been kept sufficiently in check that the high-employment budget deficit would not have risen above 1 percent of high-employment GNP. Other policy and exogenous variables were kept the same in the two simulations. In particular, the Fed was assumed to pursue the same path of

---

that *causes* a reduction in demand. The former occurs as a result of expansionary fiscal policy, whereas the latter occurs as a result of contractionary monetary policy.

Another possibility is that the prospect of large future deficits creates expectations of higher future interest rates that feed back into current long-term rates, raising them, discouraging investment, and depressing the economy. Although this scenario is theoretically possible, we have seen little evidence that suggests it is quantitatively important (cf., Alan S. Blinder, "The Message in the Models," in Hulten and Sawhill, eds., *The Legacy of Reaganomics*).

23. See Wayne Vroman, "DRI Model Simulations of Macroeconomic Performance in the 1980s," Changing Domestic Priorities Discussion Paper (Washington, D.C.: The Urban Institute, February 1984). For a similar exercise using three different models, see Blinder, "The Message in the Models," in Hulten and Sawhill, eds., *The Legacy of Reaganomics*.

M1, hence tighter fiscal policy was not offset by easier monetary policy. Details of these alternative policy assumptions can be found in Appendix A.

Real receipts and expenditures in the two simulations are compared in table 9. These data show that the Reagan administration's tax cuts are much larger than they would have been if personal income taxes had simply been indexed. On the spending side, defense purchases are higher with the Reagan administration's policies, but nondefense purchases and transfers are lower. Finally, because budget deficits are larger under the Reagan administration's policies, net interest payments also are larger. Overall,

TABLE 9

DIFFERENCE BETWEEN THE REAGAN ADMINISTRATION'S FISCAL POLICY AND A LESS EXPANSIONARY POLICY
(Billions of 1982 dollars)

	1981	*1982*	*1983*	*1984*	*1986*	*1988*
Receipts						
Personal	−1.6	−11.5	−34.3	−40.2	−30.9	−21.2
Corporate	−4.9	−18.6	−28.8	−36.9	−47.8	−50.2
Other	0.3	0.2	1.5	3.4	4.1	1.4
Total receipts	−6.2	−29.9	−61.6	−73.7	−74.6	−70.0
Expenditures						
Purchases						
Defense	0.0	3.5	8.8	14.7	22.6	31.2
Nondefense	0.1	−0.4	−5.5	−8.8	−9.0	−9.6
	0.1	3.1	3.3	5.9	13.6	21.6
Transfers						
To persons	−0.2	−4.7	−6.9	−15.5	−14.8	−18.2
To state and local governments	−1.5	−8.7	−10.1	−10.2	−13.0	−19.1
	−1.7	−13.4	−17.0	−25.7	−27.8	−37.3
Net interest paid	0.3	1.1	5.0	13.5	35.5	57.1
Total expenditures	−1.4	−9.3	−8.6	−6.3	21.4	41.4
Deficit	4.7	20.6	53.0	67.5	96.0	111.5
High-employment deficit (6% unemployment rate)	6.4	26.7	67.5	84.1	106.0	111.2
Weighted stimulus[a]	6.6	29.5	70.0	81.7	96.0	100.4
GNP	3.5	2.8	20.7	36.2	36.0	23.1

SOURCE: Simulations of the DRI model.

NOTE: Entries may not add to totals due to rounding.

a. Assumes a multiplier of 2.0 for purchases, 1.4 for taxes and transfers, and 0.2 for interest.

expenditures are slightly lower under the Reagan administration's policies through 1984 but become larger in the second half of the decade.

Table 9 shows that both the actual budget deficit and the standardized budget deficit are significantly higher after 1982 under the Reagan administration's program. Neither of these measures is, however, a fully satisfactory measure of the differential fiscal stimulus provided by that program. Although the standardized deficit offers the advantage over the actual budget deficit of controlling for different economic conditions in the two simulations, it has the offsetting disadvantage that it standardizes at a level of GNP that is very far from the actual level of GNP in the earlier years of each simulation and hence exaggerates the differential stimulus actually being provided.[24]

A more serious objection to using the budget deficit as a measure of fiscal stimulus is the fact that different components of the budget provide different amounts of fiscal stimulus. DRI reports, for example, a multiplier after eight quarters of a sustained policy change of about 2 for government purchases, and of about 1.4 for personal tax cuts and transfers.[25] Because a portion of net interest payments is really a restoration of principal to offset the effects of inflation on the real value of bond holdings, and because interest probably goes to people with high savings propensities and high marginal tax rates, there may be very little stimulus from larger interest payments.

To capture these differential fiscal impacts, we have calculated a measure of weighted fiscal stimulus to show the effect on real GNP of the net differences between the Reagan administration's fiscal policy and our tighter alternative policy. Assuming we are correct that interest outlays have a much smaller multiplier than taxes or spending, the overall multiplier declines from 1.4 in 1982 to 0.9 in 1988 with the growing importance

---

24. To the extent that tax receipts rise faster than income, the tax receipts differential measured at a relatively low level of unemployment is larger than the differential measured at a higher level of unemployment. Outlays are much less sensitive to economic activity, but if countercyclical spending would have been greater under a different administration, the high-employment comparison somewhat understates the outlay differential. Nevertheless, the receipts effects are larger, and the net effect of measuring the budget at a lower level of standardized economic activity is to reduce the standardized deficit differential between Reagan policies and our alternative policy.

25. The multiplier is the amount by which GNP changes per dollar-change in a given tax or expenditure category, assuming (1) an accommodative monetary policy to keep interest rates unchanged and (2) sufficient economic slack to permit real output to grow without inflation. The size of the multiplier is a function of how much additional spending is induced by the initial change. If, for example, all of the increased disposable income provided by a tax cut is saved, there will be no induced spending. If some is spent, however, there will be successive rounds of induced spending. Government purchases have a larger multiplier because they provide immediate and direct stimulus as well as subsequent induced stimulus.

of interest outlays in the deficit.[26] The actual increase in real GNP is less than this measure of fiscal stimulus because monetary policy was not accommodative and some fiscal stimulus was crowded out by higher interest rates. In fact, the differential fiscal stimulus provided by the Reagan administration's fiscal policy, although positive, is quite negligible throughout the 1981–1982 recession. In 1983, when the Fed allowed the money supply to grow rapidly, fiscal policy provided some modest additional stimulus to fuel the recovery. By 1984, its effects were still greater, increasing the level of GNP by about $36 billion—1 percent above what it otherwise would have been (table 10).

Changing the Composition of Output

Table 10 provides data on how the composition of output differs between our simulation of the Reagan administration's fiscal policies and our

TABLE 10

Estimated Impact of the Reagan Administration's Fiscal Policy
on the Level and Composition of Output
(Billions of 1982 dollars)

	1982	*1983*	*1984*	*1986*	*1988*
Real GNP	2.8	20.7	36.2	36.0	23.1
(percentage difference)	(0.1)	(0.7)	(1.1)	(1.0)	(0.6)
Consumption	3.7	20.9	36.3	44.5	54.2
Investment					
Business	4.5	12.7	22.1	33.1	28.4
Residential	−0.3	−3.8	−12.2	−20.8	−26.1
Inventory	0.0	4.1	9.2	10.3	14.8
	4.2	13.0	19.1	22.6	17.1
Government purchases					
Federal	2.9	2.7	4.7	11.6	20.3
State and local	−7.0	−10.8	−11.8	−15.1	−20.4
	−4.1	−8.1	−7.1	−3.5	−0.1
Net exports	−1.1	−5.1	−12.1	−27.5	−48.1

Source: Authors' calculations based on simulations using the DRI model.

Note: All entries represent the difference between the level of variable under the Reagan administration's polices less the level under the alternative, less expansionary policy discussed in the text.

---

26. The multiplier is calculated by dividing the weighted stimulus by the actual budget deficit to standardize at the actual level of economic activity.

alternative, more conservative fiscal policy. These data show that consumption and investment are higher under the Reagan administration's fiscal policy than they would have been under our assumed alternative. However, residential fixed investment (housing), net exports, and state and local government purchases are all substantially lower under the Reagan administration's fiscal program. The contrast between nonresidential fixed investment (business plant and equipment) and residential fixed investment shows that the business tax cuts were effective in shielding much business investment from the effects of higher interest rates and in diverting investment from housing into business investment.

Because the model assumes that the cuts in grants to state and local governments result in lower state and local government purchases of goods and services, there is little net crowding out by the government sector as a whole. However, if state and local governments increase their borrowing or raise taxes to maintain their purchases above the forecast levels, as they seem to have done,[27] we would expect to see more crowding out of other spending than our simulation shows. Similarly, had a business tax cut been part of our alternative fiscal policy,[28] the net stimulus to plant and equipment attributable to Reagan policies would have been smaller and there would have been relatively more crowding out of interest-sensitive spending.

These results, which attribute both greater output and a change in the composition of that output to the Reagan fiscal program, assume that the Fed would have kept money growth the same even if fiscal policy had been less expansionary. However, if the Fed would have accommodated a tighter fiscal policy with an easier monetary policy, no short-run net stimulus can be attributed to Reagan fiscal policies; their effect was only to alter the composition of output in the ways we have described.

Longer-Run Impact on Savings and Investment

In the longer run, as the economy approaches high employment, demand stimulus has diminishing effects in increasing output—a point made forcefully by supply-siders. Fiscal stimulus at high employment simply drives up interest rates or creates inflation, depending on whether the Fed keeps money tight or partially finances the deficit with money creation. While the risk of reigniting inflation is higher when the economy is at high

---

27. See George E. Peterson, "Federalism and the States," in John L. Palmer and Isabel V. Sawhill, eds., *The Reagan Record: An Assessment of America's Changing Domestic Priorities* (Cambridge, Mass: Ballinger Publishing Company, 1984), pp. 217–260.

28. The budget proposed by the outgoing Carter administration did include a business tax cut designed to stimulate investment.

employment, the Fed keeps indicating that it will risk higher interest rates rather than inflation. Thus, unless there is an unprecedented increase in saving, the stimulus to investment from the business tax cuts is likely to be counterbalanced by the discouragement from higher interest rates. In addition, the strength of the dollar will probably keep the traded goods sector weak even when the rest of the economy is healthy.

Table 11 presents historical data on net saving and investment since 1951 and our simulation results through 1988. These data show quite dramatically that even if (1) private saving recovers from its early-1980s low level to its historical average of about 7 percent of GNP, (2) residential investment is kept at a level well below its historical average, and (3) state and local government surpluses and net foreign capital inflows are huge by historical standards, federal government borrowing needs will still crowd out business investment and keep it well below its historical average of about 3 percent of GNP.

TABLE 11

Net Saving and Investment, 1951–1988
(*Percentage of GNP*)

	1951–1960	1961–1970	1971–1980	1981–1983	1984–1988[a]
Net saving	6.4	7.0	6.1	3.3	5.4
Net private saving	7.1	7.9	7.0	5.7	7.0
Personal	4.7	4.7	4.9	4.0	4.1
Net business	2.4	3.2	2.1	1.7	2.9
Government surplus or deficit	−0.4	−0.4	−0.9	−2.8	−3.5
Federal government	−0.2	−0.5	−1.9	−4.1	−5.1
State and local	−0.1	0.1	1.0	1.3	1.6
Net foreign investment	−0.3	−0.5	0	0.4	1.9
Net private domestic investment	6.7	7.0	6.2	3.2	5.3
Net fixed investment	5.9	5.9	5.5	3.3	4.4
Nonresidential	2.7	3.5	3.0	2.1	2.5
Structures	1.4	1.6	1.2	—	—
Equipment	1.3	1.8	1.8	—	—
Residential	3.2	2.5	2.5	1.2	1.9
Change in inventories	0.8	1.0	0.7	−0.1	0.9
Statistical discrepancy	−0.3	0	−0.1	0.1	0.1

NOTE: Total net savings and total net investment differ by a statistical discrepancy and entries may not add to totals due to rounding.

a. Authors' simulation based on DRI model.

Conclusions

The macroeconomic policies pursued since 1979 have produced a substantial decline in inflation, a severe recession, and an unbalanced recovery. Our analysis suggests the following conclusion:

- The severity of the recession and, hence, part of the decline in inflation were unanticipated consequences of the Fed's paying too much attention to the behavior of the money supply and not enough attention to other evidence of how much its policies were choking off spending in 1981 and 1982;
- The high real interest rates and exceptionally strong dollar that have kept some sectors from participating fully in the recovery and that threaten long-term growth are a consequence of the Reagan administration's willingness to tolerate large budget deficits; and
- Unless progress is made to reduce the budget deficits, the Fed will be forced to offset continued fiscal stimulus with sustained monetary restraint, keeping real interest rates high and investment low.

In the next chapter we investigate how differently the economy would have performed in the short run if the Fed had moved more quickly to expand the money supply in the face of falling velocity and rising real interest rates and if the administration had been more concerned with preventing large budget deficits than with preserving its tax cuts. Finally, in chapter 4 we investigate whether the economy's prospects for long-term growth are on the whole better as a result of the positive effects of the administration's supply-side policies or worse as a result of the negative effects of the recession and the budget deficits.

CHAPTER 3

WAS THERE AN ALTERNATIVE TO REAGANOMICS?

In chapter 1 we argued that part of the decline in inflation between 1980 and 1983 resulted from favorable movements in the price of food, energy, and imports, which reversed the adverse price shocks that had aggravated inflation in 1979 and 1980, while the rest resulted from the economic slack associated with back-to-back recessions in 1980 and 1981-1982. In chapter 2 we argued that these recessions resulted largely from the deliberate decision by the Federal Reserve to restrain spending, and that the Fed's monetarist approach to restraining spending probably caused the 1981-1982 recession to be worse than it would have been if the Fed had given less weight to the behavior of the money supply in setting policy. In this chapter we examine alternative policies that might have been followed during this period; our aim is to determine whether some of the high costs associated with the fight against inflation could have been avoided, and, if so, how much less inflation would have come down.

Alternative Macroeconomic Policies

Given the fears about spiraling inflation in late 1979 and early 1980, some tightening by the Fed was probably inevitable and a recession in 1980 was probably unavoidable. Also, monetary policy affects spending with a lag, and some of the effects of tight money in 1980 might have carried over into 1981. Nevertheless, the Fed did begin to curtail money growth early in 1981 (see figure 5); if it had not, the economy might have continued its recovery rather than going into another recession.

To see whether a recession was inevitable in 1981 and by how much inflation could have been brought down without so severe a recession, we analyzed three alternative policies that might have been pursued after 1980:

1. An easier monetary policy (faster growth in the money supply beginning in 1981);
2. An easier monetary policy combined with a tighter fiscal policy (less government spending and smaller tax cuts in order to avoid large deficits); and
3. An incomes policy (direct action to moderate wage and price increases).

To examine the first two alternatives, we conducted simulations of specific alternative policies using the DRI model. The advantages and disadvantages of such an approach that were discussed in chapter 2 apply here as well. The "easier monetary" alternative assumes actual fiscal policy and an easier monetary policy beginning in 1981 aimed at restoring high employment as quickly as possible. The "easier monetary, tighter fiscal" alternative assumes a similar monetary policy and the tighter fiscal policy discussed in chapter 2. Table 12 provides a comparison of some key policy and performance variables from these simulations with their actual (through 1983) and simulated (1984–1988) values assuming no change in policy after 1983 ("actual" policy). For completeness, we include data from the fiscal policy simulation discussed in chapter 2 (the "tighter fiscal" alternative), but because this policy combination is more restrictive than actual policies, it is given little further attention in this chapter.[1] Alternative 3 does not lend itself to a simulation and our discussion is thus more qualitative.

Alternative 1: An Easier Monetary Policy

To see what difference it would have made if the Fed had been more concerned with nurturing the economic recovery that was under way at the beginning of 1981 than with slowing the rate of growth of the money supply, we let the money supply grow as rapidly as the model would allow, beginning in 1981, with the goal of reaching high employment (6 percent unemployment) as rapidly as possible. Figure 9 compares real output (GNP), interest rates (three-month Treasury bills), inflation (CPI), and unemployment for this simulation, our simulation of actual policies, and the administration's January 1984 forecast.

Even rapid expansion of the money supply does not prevent a mild growth recession in 1981, given the lagged effects of earlier monetary re-

---

1. Further details on all the simulations can be found in appendix A.

straint, but unemployment hardly rises at all from its 1980 rate of 7 percent, and the economy reaches high employment in 1984 with an inflation rate less than two points higher than in the simulation of actual policies (figure 9 and table 12).[2] Keeping the economy at a 6 percent unemployment rate results in an inflation rate slightly more than two points higher in 1988 compared with the rate experienced under "actual" policies, where unemployment falls only to 7.1 percent. An easier monetary policy produces higher incomes and lower interest rates, hence budget deficits are smaller. The combination of lower interest rates and less addition to debt means that the federal government's interest outlays are lower; so, therefore, is the high-employment budget deficit, even though the exogenous components of fiscal policy are the same in the two simulations.

Although the specifics of any simulation should be treated with a healthy dose of skepticism, these results confirm our observation that the reversal of the adverse price shocks of the 1970s and the economic slack arising from Fed restraint in 1979 and 1980 probably would have checked the rise in inflation and brought it down below double-digit rates in the 1980s, even without a severe recession in 1981 and 1982. These results also point out the importance of poor economic performance and high interest rates in contributing to the deficit problem that is an enduring legacy of economic policy in the Reagan years.

Although it may be unrealistic to think that the Fed would have been willing to expand the money supply as rapidly in 1981 as this simulation requires, we have seen that the recession was probably deeper than the Fed had anticipated as a result of the unexpected decline in velocity in 1982. In fact, our simulation results imply that if the Fed had anticipated and chosen to accommodate this drop in velocity earlier, the 1981–1982 recession would have been avoided. This accommodation could have happened more or less automatically if the Fed had been focusing more on interest rates and less on the money supply in 1981 and therefore had expanded the money supply to keep real interest rates from rising as much as they did. However, such accommodation would have run counter to monetarist views, and although the Fed has never operated entirely according to monetarist doctrine, its own inclinations in that direction may have been reinforced by the strong influence of this viewpoint within the Reagan administration in 1981.

---

2. It might be more accurate to describe this policy as moving strong monetary growth forward from 1982–1983 to 1981–1982. The average annual rate of growth in the money supply from 1982 to 1984 is 7.4 percent in our easier monetary policy simulation, but 8.2 percent in our simulation of actual policies. The easier monetary policy simulation shows more rapid growth after 1984, but it also shows a persistently lower unemployment rate.

TABLE 12

POLICY AND PERFORMANCE INDICATORS UNDER ALTERNATIVE MONETARY AND FISCAL POLICY SIMULATIONS, 1981–1988

	1981	1982	1983	1984	1986	1988
Real GNP (Billions of 1982 dollars)						
Actual	3,130.0	3,073.2	3,176.4	3,352.3	3,566.8	3,806.0
Difference from actual (percent)						
Easier monetary	3.8	9.2	9.7	6.7	6.8	7.4
Tighter fiscal	0.0	−0.1	−0.7	−1.1	−1.0	−0.6
Easier monetary, tighter fiscal	2.8	6.2	7.4	5.0	5.7	5.6
Unemployment Rate[a]						
Actual	7.6	9.7	9.6	7.6	7.3	7.1
Difference from actual (percentage points)						
Easier monetary	−0.5	−2.5	−3.0	−1.5	−1.2	−1.1
Tighter fiscal	0.0	0.0	0.2	0.3	0.1	−0.2
Easier monetary, tighter fiscal	−0.4	−1.7	−2.3	−1.4	−1.2	−1.1
Inflation Rate[b]						
Actual	10.3	6.2	3.2	4.9	5.2	5.9
Difference from actual (percentage points)						
Easier monetary	0.4	1.4	2.1	1.7	1.9	1.9
Tighter fiscal	0.0	0.0	0.0	−0.2	0.0	0.2
Easier monetary, tighter fiscal	0.3	1.0	1.5	1.5	2.0	1.9
Interest Rate[c]						
Actual	14.0	10.6	8.6	8.8	9.7	9.2
Difference from actual (percentage points)						
Easier monetary	−8.1	−7.2	−0.9	−2.9	−3.5	−2.9
Tighter fiscal	0.0	−0.2	−1.2	−2.2	−3.4	−3.8
Easier monetary, tighter fiscal	−7.0	−5.8	−3.2	−3.4	−4.9	−3.6

M1

	436.7	475.7	523.4	557.0	627.0	699.0
Actual						
Difference from actual (percent)						
Easier monetary	5.7	8.1	6.6	6.6	9.5	13.2
Tighter fiscal	0.0	−0.1	−0.1	0.0	−0.1	0.1
Easier monetary, tighter fiscal	4.6	5.8	5.6	5.3	8.3	10.7
M1 Growth Rate						
Actual	5.1	8.9	10.0	6.4	5.8	5.6
Difference from actual (percentage points)						
Easier monetary	6.1	2.5	−1.5	0.0	1.9	2.0
Tighter fiscal	0.0	0.0	0.0	0.1	0.0	0.1
Easier monetary, tighter fiscal	4.9	1.2	−0.1	−0.3	1.3	1.0
Deficit/GNP[d]						
Actual	2.1	4.8	5.5	4.9	5.3	4.9
Difference from actual (percentage points)						
Easier monetary	−1.0	−3.8	−4.2	−3.1	−3.3	−3.7
Tighter fiscal	−0.1	−0.7	−1.6	−2.0	−2.7	−3.0
Easier monetary, tighter fiscal	−0.9	−3.3	−5.0	−4.6	−5.3	−5.2
High-Employment Deficit/GNP[e]						
Actual	0.6	1.8	2.7	3.1	3.7	3.3
Difference from actual (percentage points)						
Easier monetary	−0.5	−1.6	−1.8	−1.8	−2.3	−2.7
Tighter fiscal	−0.2	−0.8	−2.0	−2.4	−2.9	−2.9
Easier monetary, tighter fiscal	−0.5	−1.7	−3.1	−3.4	−4.2	−4.3

SOURCE: Authors' simulations based on the DRI model.

a. Civilian unemployment rate.
b. Consumer price index.
c. Three-month Treasury bill rate.
d. NIA budget deficit.
e. NIA budget at 6 percent unemployment.

FIGURE 9

ECONOMIC INDICATORS: ACTUAL POLICY COMPARED WITH
AN EASIER MONETARY POLICY

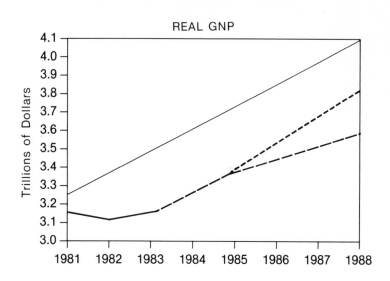

REAL GNP

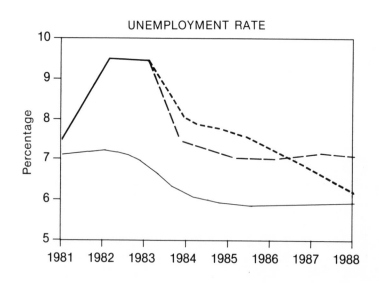

UNEMPLOYMENT RATE

——— Actual
——— Easier monetary policy, actual fiscal policy simulation
·------ Administration forecast, January 1984
—— —— Urban Institute/DRI simulation of actual policies

FIGURE 9 (Cont.)

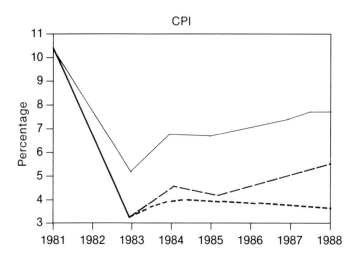

CPI

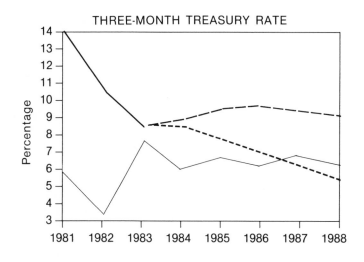

THREE-MONTH TREASURY RATE

——————— Actual
——————— Easier monetary policy, actual fiscal policy simulation
- - - - - - - Administration forecast, January 1984
—-——-——- Urban Institute/DRI simulation of actual policies

SOURCE: Office of Management and Budget, *Budget of the United States
Government, Fiscal Year 1985* (Washington, D.C.: Government
Printing Office, 1984), pp. 2–10 and 2–11, and authors' simulations
based on DRI model.

Alternative 2: An Easier Monetary Policy Combined with a
Tighter Fiscal Policy

Even if the Fed had focused more on interest rates, it might still have
been so concerned about the stimulus to the economy from large budget
deficits that it would have been fearful of allowing the money supply to
expand rapidly as well. However, if there had been smaller budget deficits
and a weaker economy, the Fed might have allowed greater money growth.
An easier monetary policy and a tighter fiscal policy would have been more
like the policies of the 1970s, and such a combination might actually have
been followed if Jimmy Carter had been reelected or if Congress had re-
jected the Reagan administration's budget and tax program in 1981.

In our simulation of this alternative, we used the same fiscal policy
assumptions we used in the tighter fiscal policy alternative of chapter 2. In
broad outline, this policy included indexing of the personal income tax
beginning in 1981, no business tax cut, a smaller defense buildup, and
smaller cuts in nondefense expenditures, all aimed at keeping the high-
employment budget deficit within 1 percent of GNP. Taking into account
lingering fears of an overly expansionary monetary policy in 1981, we did
not allow M1 to rise quite so rapidly in this simulation as we did in the
easier monetary alternative, but the rate of growth of the money supply is
still considerably higher in 1981 than the Fed actually allowed (see table
12).

This combination of an easier monetary and a tighter fiscal policy
does not keep the economy from suffering a serious recession, but that
recession is much less severe than the one we actually experienced. Unemployment rises, but not above 8 percent. With a less severe recession, inflation falls substantially, but once again not so far as under actual policies.
The high-employment budget shows a surplus after 1983 and the actual
budget is practically balanced (see table 12 and figure 10).

As before, these results are based on specific policy assumptions and a
specific model and should therefore not be taken too literally in all their
details. Nevertheless, they illustrate the general effects to be expected from
a whole range of policies that fall under the general rubric of "gradualism"—in contrast to the "cold turkey" approach actually followed between 1980 and 1982.

The advantage of gradualism is that it gives people additional time to
adjust to a more slowly growing economy and thus imposes less individual
hardship. There are likely to be fewer bankruptcies, less need to renegoti-
ate existing collective bargaining or loan agreements, and more widespread sharing of the costs of unemployment. Table 13, for example, compares the income losses that would have been suffered if Alternatives 1 or 2
had been followed with the losses calculated in chapter 1 from actual poli-

cies. Under Alternative 1, 70 percent of the cumulative loss between 1980 and 1986 and two-thirds of the losses incurred between 1981 and 1983 would have been avoided. Even under Alternative 2, nearly 60 percent of the cumulative losses and nearly half of the 1981–1983 losses could have been avoided.

Although the decline in inflation under each of these alternatives is substantial and is achieved at a much lower cost than the decline under actual policies, it is still smaller than the decline under actual policies. In addition, the severity of the 1981–1982 recession might have resulted in wage and work rule concessions or management efficiencies that contributed to the decline in inflation and would not have been effected by more gradualist policies. Moreover, there was no guarantee that public opinion and political pressures would have allowed gradualism to work. The costs of a gradualist policy are incurred before the benefits become apparent, making it politically difficult to stay the anti-inflation course.

Alternative 3: An Incomes Policy

Given the difficulties with both gradualism and cold turkey policies, some economists have long favored an incomes policy as the best way to minimize the costs associated with policies that operate solely by restricting demand, even though controls have their own costs. Specific proposals for a tax-based incomes policy (providing rewards to people practicing wage or price restraint) surfaced at the end of the Carter administration, and most post-World War II administrations instituted some form of wage-price controls or guidelines. Unfortunately, available evidence suggests that incomes policies have had only a temporary effect in slowing inflation, which tends to decline when controls are put in place but to rise once they are removed.[3]

Pessimism about the effectiveness of incomes policies should be tempered, however, with the recognition that they have been used in the past more to supplant than to supplement monetary and fiscal restraint. Thus, incomes policies might have worked better after 1979, when there was a much greater commitment to monetary restraint.

This discussion of alternative ways of dealing with inflation has significance for the future as well as the past. Despite the substantial reduction in inflation achieved so far, inflation has not been eliminated. Inflation in the mid-1980s could easily exceed 5 percent, a rate that would have seemed intolerable barely fifteen years ago. To reduce inflation further will require

---

3. For a review of the evidence on the effectiveness of incomes policies, see Isabel V. Sawhill, "Incomes Policies," Urban Institute Discussion Paper (Washington, D.C.: The Urban Institute, 1981).

FIGURE 10

ECONOMIC INDICATORS: ACTUAL POLICY COMPARED WITH
AN EASIER MONETARY AND A TIGHTER FISCAL POLICY

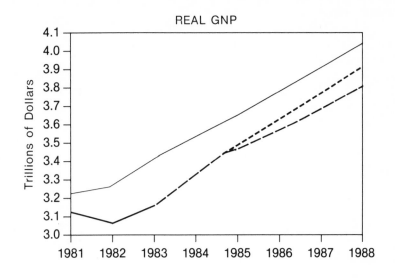

REAL GNP

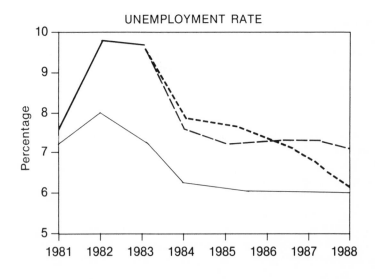

UNEMPLOYMENT RATE

———— Actual
———— Easier monetary policy, tighter fiscal policy simulation
·------ Administration forecast, January 1984
----- Urban Institute/DRI simulation of actual policies

FIGURE 10 (Cont.)

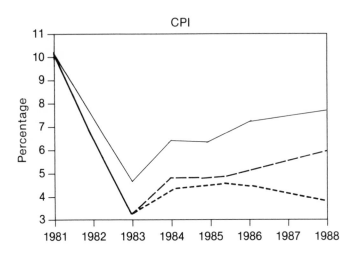

CPI

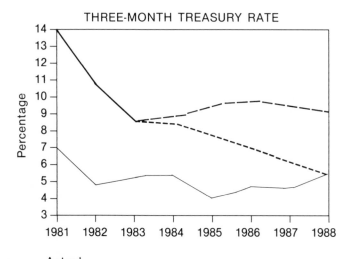

THREE-MONTH TREASURY RATE

——— Actual
——— Easier monetary policy, tighter fiscal policy simulation
·----· Administration forecast, January 1984
——— Urban Institute/DRI simulation of actual policies

SOURCE: Office of Management and Budget, *Budget of the United States Government, Fiscal Year 1985* (Washington, D.C.: Government Printing Office, 1984), pp. 2–10 and 2–11, and authors' simulations based on the DRI model.

TABLE 13

COSTS OF THE 1981–1982 RECESSION

| | Losses in After-Tax Income (1982 dollars) | |
	Per Household	Per Person
Amount by which actual income is lower than what would have been earned with unemployment at 6 percent		
1980	528	187
1981–1983	3,309	1,187
Projected, 1984–1986[a]	2,042	746
Cumulative, 1980–1986	5,879	2,120
Cumulative incremental losses due to the severity of the recession compared with an easier monetary policy alternative (Alternative 1)[b]		
1980	0	0
1981–1983	2,181	782
Projected, 1984–1986	1,954	714
Cumulative, 1980–1986	4,135	1,496
Cumulative incremental losses attributable to the severity of the recession compared with an easier monetary and tighter fiscal policy alternative (Alternative 2)[c]		
1980	0	0
1981–1983	1,557	559
Projected, 1984–1986	1,868	683
Cumulative, 1980–1986	3,425	1,232

SOURCE: Courtenay Slater, "Income Loss Due to the Recession," Changing Domestic Priorities Discussion Paper (Washington, D.C.: The Urban Institute, January 1984); authors' simulations based on the DRI model.

a. Assumes output grows according to the administration's January 1984 economic assumptions in Office of Management and Budget, *Budget of the United States Government, Fiscal Year 1985* (Washington, D.C.: Government Printing Office, 1984). Since the Slater calculation of potential GNP is below the 3.2 percent annual trend calculated by the U.S. Department of Commerce that is implicit in the Reagan administration's forecast, actual output crosses Slater potential in 1986, before unemployment reaches 6 percent.

b. Calculated by applying the ratio of the cumulative unemployment gap in the easier monetary/fiscal policy simulation to the cumulative unemployment gap in a simulation of actual policies. The unemployment gap is calculated using 6 percent as the high-employment unemployment rate.

c. Calculated as in (b), but using the unemployment gap from the easier monetary/ tighter fiscal policy simulation.

more luck, an extended period of economic slack, another recession, or experimentation with new kinds of incomes policies that are more successful than those of the past.

Some economists believe that wages and prices are quite inflexible, especially in a downward direction, with the result that the economy is prone to inflation even when unemployment remains relatively high.[4] If this is the case, unless the wage- and price-setting institutions that produce this inflexibility (for example, multiyear union contracts) are changed, the only way to maintain price stability over the long run would be to maintain permanent slack in the economy. Perhaps one of the intangible benefits of the experience the nation has just gone through will be greater willingness to change some of these institutional practices.

The Gains from Lower Inflation

Has the reduction in inflation that has been achieved so far been worth the high cost paid in terms of lost output and employment? Is it worth incurring additional costs of this sort to lower inflation still further?

Notwithstanding the widespread belief that inflation is a major problem, there is remarkably little analytical evidence on the economic costs of inflation. One estimate does indicate that the eventual consequences of lowering inflation by five points would be to permanently raise the level of real GNP by 1 percent.[5] If this estimate were correct, the temporary costs of the last recession would be nearly counterbalanced by the permanent gain in output.[6] However, the costs attributed to inflation in these calculations arise as a result of financial regulations and a tax code that lead to increasing inefficiencies with rising inflation. For example, effective corporate tax rates may vary with inflation, leading to considerable uncertainty about after-tax rates of return on investment. Recent financial and

---

4. The argument goes as follows: Even at high employment, changing patterns of demand will lead to expansion in some sectors and contraction in others. If price increases in those sectors experiencing rising demand are not offset by price reductions in those sectors with falling demand because of wage and price rigidities, the general price level will rise. See, for example, James Tobin, "Inflation and Unemployment," *American Economic Review*, vol. 62, no. 1 (March 1972), pp. 1–18; and Arthur M. Okun, *Prices and Quantities: A Macroeconomic Analysis* (Washington, D.C.: The Brookings Institution, 1981).

5. The estimate is from Gordon and King, "The Output Cost of Disinflation," and is based on Stanley Fischer, "Towards an Understanding of the Costs of Inflation: II," *Carnegie-Rochester Conference Series on Public Policy*, vol. 15 (1981), pp. 5–42.

6. The output costs of $970 billion calculated in chapter 1 (table 5) assume a potential GNP of about $3.3 trillion in 1982. A permanent annual gain of 1 percent—$33 billion—in potential GNP has a present value of $660 billion, when discounted at a rate 5 percent higher than the rate of growth of potential, and $1.32 trillion when discounted at a rate 2.5 percent higher than the rate of growth of potential.

tax reforms like allowing interest to be paid on checking accounts and lowering business taxes have reduced many of these inefficiencies and have lowered the costs associated with inflation accordingly. Further reform could reduce them still more, but as long as any remain, inflation will continue to impose some economic costs.

The costs just discussed are costs associated with high rates of inflation. There will be additional costs if high rates of inflation bring with them greater variability in the rate of inflation, because it will be more difficult for households and firms to disentangle changes in relative prices from changes in the general price level, increasing the possibility that resources will be misallocated as a result of misread price signals. To our knowledge, no estimates of these costs have been made.[7]

A popular argument against inflation is that it makes everyone poorer by reducing purchasing power, but this is wrong. Inflation leads to increases in the prices of what people buy, but it also means increases in the prices of what they sell, including their labor. Inflation may hurt some groups relative to others, but it does not make the nation as a whole worse off (beyond the effects already discussed). Union workers may gain at the expense of nonunion workers; retirees dependent on Social Security may gain relative to those dependent on their own savings; and people on incomes that are fixed in money terms are certain to lose out to people who are well organized to make sure their incomes rise along with inflation. Thus, inflation may act as an arbitrary redistributional tax. It may also be psychologically and politically unsettling, and these consequences may be as important as the economic costs.

There is one more real and calculable cost of inflation: it induces policymakers to fight inflation, and the costs of fighting inflation are high. For this reason, it is worth trying hard to preserve the gains that have been made against inflation over the past few years, but it may not be worth trying for a further significant reduction by incurring another recession. No administration can openly admit that it has adopted a policy of benign neglect toward the existing level of inflation for fear of the political consequences. But neither is any administration in the mid-1980s likely to adopt a program that tries to eliminate inflation *entirely*.

The Legacy of the Recession

One reason any administration will be reluctant to accept another recession as the price of lowering inflation still further is that many of the effects of the previous recession are still with us. For one thing, average

---

7. See Fischer, "Towards an Understanding of the Costs of Inflation," pp. 33–36.

economic performance for the decade of the 1980s will be weak in many respects compared with that of the 1970s, even with strong performance in the latter part of the decade. For another, large interest payments on the debt accumulated during the recession are now embedded in the high-employment budget, seriously aggravating the deficit problem. Finally, the loss of investment during the recession means that the economy's capacity for producing goods and services will be lower through the remainder of the decade than it would have been without a recession.

Average Economic Performance

One of President Reagan's implicit promises was that the 1980s would be better than the 1970s. When we look at the economy's poor performance in the early part of the 1980s, however, it becomes apparent that the economy would have to perform extremely well for the rest of the decade to end up performing as well over the whole decade as it did during the 1970s.

Table 14 compares three economic projections for the remainder of the decade with what would be required over the same period to match the performance of the 1970s. These comparisons show that the 1980s will almost certainly be a decade of high unemployment, excess capacity, and slow growth compared with the situation in the 1970s. Inflation will be lower, but standards of living are not likely to improve as much over the 1980s as they did over the 1970s. To match the performance of the 1970s, real per capita disposable income would have to increase by 3.4 percent a year beginning in 1984, and this is far above most projections for this period.

The Budget

Table 15 provides data on the composition of the high-employment federal budget in 1979 and in 1988 under the four different combinations of monetary and fiscal policies that we have simulated. Comparing the simulation of actual policies with the simulation of an easier monetary policy that avoids a severe recession in 1981 and 1982 shows that the larger deficits associated with the recession increase interest outlays as a share of GNP by 2 percentage points, total expenditures by 2.8 percentage points, and the deficit by 2.7 percentage points.[8] With an easier monetary policy

---

8. Real high-employment GNP is higher in the easier monetary policy simulation because there is greater investment and capital formation, but the exogenous components of government spending are the same in real terms in the two simulations. Thus, the ratio of spending to GNP is different in the two simulations for some categories of spending. Similarly, income taxes are somewhat higher as a share of GNP in the easier monetary policy simulation because income tax receipts increase faster than income with progressive tax rates.

TABLE 14

WILL THE 1980s BE BETTER THAN THE 1970s?

(*Percentages*)

	1970-1979 Average	1980-1983 Average[a]	Required 1984-1989 Average[b]	Projected 1984-1989 average		
				Data Resources, Inc.[c]	Administration	Congressional Budget Office
Civilian unemployment rate	6.2	8.5	4.7	7.5	7.0[d]	7.0
Capacity utilization rate	81.8	76.4	85.4	82.7	NA	NA
Inflation rate	6.5	7.2	6.0	5.2	4.2[e]	4.7
Productivity growth	1.4	1.1	1.6	1.8	NA	NA
Real growth in GNP	3.2	0.9	4.7	3.4	4.2	3.8
Real growth in per capita disposable terms	2.4	0.9	3.4	1.9	NA	NA

SOURCES: Historical data from *Economic Report of the President* (Washington, D.C.: Government Printing Office, 1984), tables B-29 (p. 254), B-45 (p. 271), B-3 (p. 224), B-40 (p. 266), B-2 (p. 222), B-24 (p. 249). Projections from Data Resources, Inc. (DRI), *The Data Resources Review of the U.S. Economy, February 1984* (Lexington, Mass.: DRI, 1984); DRI, *U.S. Long-Term Review, Winter 1983–84* (Lexington, Mass.: DRI, 1983); Executive Office of the President, Office of Management and Budget, *Budget of the United States Government, FY 1985*, (Washington, D.C.: Government Printing Office, 1984); Congressional Budget Office, *The Economic Outlook: A Report to the Senate and House Committees on the Budget—Part 1*, (Washington, D.C.: Government Printing Office, 1984).

NOTES: Capacity utilization rate is for total manufacturing (Federal Reserve Board series); inflation rate is measured by year-over-year changes in the GNP implicit price deflator; productivity growth is measured by year-over-year changes in the index of output per hour of all persons in the nonfarm business sector.

NA = not available.

a. Based on preliminary data for 1983.

b. Required averages for the 1984–1989 period to make averages for that period equal to those for the 1970–1979 period.

c. The DRI February 1984 document contains projections through 1986 only. Extrapolation, based on the DRI Winter 1983–1984 document, resulted in 1987–1989 projections.

d. In its budget document, the administration publishes projected unemployment rates for the entire labor force (including resident armed forces). The 1984–1988 average unemployment rate for the entire labor force is 6.9 percent. To arrive at the average civilian unemployment rate, 0.1 percentage point was added to this figure.

TABLE 15

THE HIGH-EMPLOYMENT BUDGET UNDER ALTERNATIVE ECONOMIC POLICIES

(Percentage of GNP)

			1988		
	1979	Actual Policy	Easier Monetary/ Actual Fiscal Policy	Actual Monetary/ Tighter Fiscal Policy	Easier Monetary/ Tighter Fiscal Policy
Receipts					
Personal tax and nontax receipts	9.5	9.4	9.6	10.0	9.8
Corporate profits tax accruals	3.1	1.9	1.6	3.3	3.2
Indirect business tax accruals	1.2	1.4	1.3	1.3	1.3
Contributions for social insurance	6.6	7.9	8.0	8.0	8.0
Total receipts	20.4	20.6	20.5	22.7	22.2
Expenditures					
Purchases of goods and services					
Defense	4.6	6.4	6.1	5.6	5.4
Nondefense	2.3	2.1	2.1	2.4	2.4
Transfers	8.5	8.9	8.6	9.5	9.2
Grants-in-aid to state and local governments	3.3	2.4	2.2	2.9	2.8
Net interest paid	1.8	3.7	1.7	2.2	1.2
Other	0.6	0.4	0.4	0.5	0.3
Total expenditures	21.1	23.9	21.1	23.1	21.3
Deficit (—) or Surplus	−0.7	−3.3	−0.6	−0.4	1.0

SOURCE: Authors' calcualtions using the DRI model.

NOTE: National Income and Products Account basis assuming 6 percent unemployment. Entries may not add to totals due to rounding.

and no recession, receipts, expenditures, and the deficit (as a percentage of GNP) would have been about the same as they were in 1979.

The composition of the budget, however, would have been different from what it was in 1979, even if the recession had been avoided. A comparison of the 1979 budget with the 1988 budget under an easier monetary policy shows that the personal tax cuts of 1981 through 1983 succeeded only in holding personal income taxes constant as a share of GNP and that substantial cuts in corporate taxes were counterbalanced by increases in contributions for social insurance. On the spending side, transfers remain constant despite the program cuts of 1981, and increases in defense purchases are offset by reductions in nondefense purchases and grants-in-aid to state and local governments. Avoiding the recession keeps interest outlays at about the same percentage of GNP that they were in 1979.

The other data in table 15 show that more modest tax cuts and defense expenditure increases could also have avoided large high-employment budget deficits even with tight money and a recession, but at the cost of seeing both receipts and expenditures rise as a share of GNP. The tighter fiscal policy discussed in chapter 2 would have produced an even more severe recession, but not a continuing deficit problem. With smaller deficits throughout the recession, accumulated debt is less and interest outlays in 1988 are correspondingly smaller. However, high-employment receipts as a share of GNP rise 2.3 points as a result of rising personal income tax receipts and rising contributions for social insurance. Expenditures rise as well, with the increase coming in defense and social insurance transfers. Finally, table 15 shows that a tighter fiscal policy combined with an easier monetary policy produces a high-employment surplus by 1988 because of rising tax receipts.

Investment and Economic Capacity

An economy's capacity for producing goods and services depends on the size of its labor force, the size of its capital stock, and the efficiency with which it uses these productive inputs to produce output. Recessions may have the beneficial effect of purging an economy of its worst inefficiencies, selecting out good from bad performers, forcing managers to pay more attention to costs, and encouraging employees to work harder. The lower inflation resulting from recessions may create a better environment for business planning and investment. But there are also some negative effects. Most important, recessions reduce investment; hence the capital stock and labor productivity grow less rapidly than would be the case if there were no recession. Also, the increase in the number of people discouraged from seeking work during a recession may persist into the postrecession period because work habits and the acquisition of job-related skills have been impaired. This discouragement of work appears to be one of the reasons why the labor force grew so slowly during 1983.

Many of these costs are intangible and hard to calculate, but our simulations do allow us to discuss lost investment. Based on our simulations, total fixed investment as a share of GNP would have been about two percentage points per year higher in the 1981–1983 period under polices that avoided a severe recession. Because each of these alternative policies features lower interest rates as well as a less severe recession, not all this difference can be attributed to the effects of the recession. If the recession is assumed to have reduced investment by 1.5 points in each of these years, the capital stock in 1984 would have been about $150 billion higher if there had been no recession.[9]

In our judgment, the negative effects of the recession, especially the loss of capital formation, are important and probably outweigh the benefits of a leaner business sector and a less inflationary environment. But it is too early to be certain what the ultimate effect of the recession will be on long-term growth. In any event, the recession is only one factor affecting long-term growth, and we defer a full assessment until the next chapter.

Conclusions

The policy choices made between 1979 and 1984 marked a change from past policies. Sustained restraint of aggregate demand between 1979 and 1982, exercised largely by the Federal Reserve, produced a severe recession and a substantial decline in inflation. The combination of an expansionary fiscal policy beginning in 1981 and continued monetary restraint in the interest of controlling inflation has produced very high real interest rates, a strong dollar, and an unbalanced economic recovery. Our simulations of alternative policies suggest the following:

1. Much of the severity of the recession could have been avoided with less restrictive macroeconomic policies—whatever the mix of monetary and fiscal policies;
2. Inflation would still have come down, but not so much; and
3. Large budget deficits, high interest rates, and a recovery in which some sectors are left out could have been avoided if there had been a different *mix* of monetary and fiscal policies—one more like that of the past with less fiscal stimulus but more monetary stimulus.

---

9. High-employment GNP averaged about $3.3 trillion (in 1982 dollars) between 1981 and 1983. An investment loss equal to 1.5 percent of GNP for each of these three years translates into a loss in capital formation of $148.5 billion.

TABLE 16

COMPARING EFFECTS OF ACTUAL POLICY WITH THOSE OF A LESS RESTRICTIVE
MACROECONOMIC POLICY, COMBINING A TIGHTER FISCAL POLICY WITH AN
EASIER MONETARY POLICY, 1981–1984

1984	Actual Policy[a]	Alternative Policy[b]	Difference
Inflation rate (CPI)	4.5	5.9	+1.4
Unemployment rate (civilian)	7.5	6.1	−1.4
Real after-tax family income (1982 dollars)	21,038[c]	21,143[c]	+105
High-employment budget deficit (−) or surplus ($ billions)	−120.8	13.8	−134.6
Three-month Treasury bill rate (percent)	9.8	6.0	−3.8
Net exports ($ billions)	−67	−28	+39
Net interest payments on federal debt ($ billions)	116	65	−51

a. Except for family incomes, data are from July 1984 DRI Forecast, *Review of the U.S. Economy*, (Lexington, Mass.: DRI, July 1984).

b. Except for family incomes, entries are calculated by applying the percentage difference between the value from our simulation of actual policies and our simulation of an easier monetary policy and a tighter fiscal policy to the value from the July 1984 DRI forecast.

c. Marilyn Moon and Isabel V. Sawhill, "Family Incomes," in John L. Palmer and Isabel V. Sawhill, eds., *The Reagan Record: An Assessment of America's Changing Domestic Priorities* (Cambridge, Mass.: Ballinger Publishing Company, 1984), table 10.5, p. 329.

Table 16 compares the economy in 1984 with where it might have been if these alternative policies had been followed. The table shows that inflation would have been about a point and a half higher and unemployment about a point and half lower. Real disposable family income would have been slightly higher.[10] The high-employment budget is balanced, interest rates are lower, the trade deficit is much smaller, and interest obligations on the debt are considerably lower.

In this chapter we have focused primarily on how economic policy choices made between 1979 and 1984 have altered the economy's short-run performance from what it would have been if more conventional policies had been followed. In the next chapter we ask what difference these choices have made for long-term growth.

---

10. Pretax income is considerably higher, but our alternative policy assumes higher taxes.

CHAPTER 4

PROSPECTS FOR LONG-TERM GROWTH

The economic recovery that began at the end of 1982 brought with it renewed optimism about the future. Although supply-side economics had met with only limited success in the short run, its longer-term potential was likely to be greater. New incentives for business investment, tax cuts providing greater rewards for individual effort and savings, and deregulation are unlikely to have much impact in the midst of a recession when there is much unused capacity. But they can be expected to produce higher investment, more work effort, and greater efficiency once the economy is operating closer to its potential. The net effect of these supply-side effects is almost certainly positive;[1] their magnitude and significance are more debatable. Also at issue is the extent to which any positive effects will be neutralized if large deficits should absorb an increasing share of the nation's saving.

Once the economy is operating at full capacity with all resources employed, its rate of growth depends on the rate of capital formation, growth of the labor force, and improvements in the efficiency with which resources are used. In this chapter, we examine the impact of the Reagan administration's policies on each of these variables. We begin with a review of the reasons for the recent slowdown in productivity growth on the grounds that an accurate diagnosis of the problem should be the first step in effecting a cure. We then look at whether there is any evidence of a short-run supply-side response to the Reagan administration's policies in the data for the

---

1. A priori, the effects could be either positive or negative. A tax reduction increases the after-tax income associated with any given level of work effort or savings. Thus, people can achieve the same target level of income by working or saving less than before. Conversely, because the reward for working an extra hour or saving an extra dollar has increased, people have a greater incentive to undertake these activities. The net effect of a tax reduction depends on the relative strength of these opposing income and incentive effects.

73

1981–1983 period. Finally, we discuss the extent to which capital formation, the supply of labor, and overall efficiency are likely to be favorably
affected by the Reagan administration's policies over the longer run.

The Slowdown in Economic Growth and Productivity

Productivity growth is crucial for generating a rising standard of
living. Output per capita can grow as a result of rising labor force participation or a longer work week, with their attendant sacrifice of less time
for leisure or work in the home. Output per hour and a rising real wage,
however, can increase only as a result of capital accumulation or increases
in overall economic efficiency (what economists call "multifactor
productivity.)"

Over the entire period from 1948 to 1981, the average annual rate of
growth of labor productivity (output per hour) was 2.4 percent (table 17).
Together with modest growth in labor force participation, this strong productivity growth more than offset a steady reduction in hours worked, and
growth in real output per capita averaged 1.9 percent per year. The Bureau
of Labor Statistics (BLS) attributes about 40 percent of the growth in labor
productivity during this period to capital accumulation and the remaining
60 percent to rising multifactor productivity.

Output per capita rose especially rapidly between 1948 and 1973, almost exclusively as a result of rising labor productivity. The BLS attributes
two-thirds of the 3 percent per year growth in labor productivity to rising
multifactor productivity and one-third to capital accumulation. Labor
force participation hardly increased at all, and hours worked declined at a
0.8 percent average annual rate. As a result, output per capita rose at an
average annual rate of 2.2 percent. Interestingly, 60 percent of the growth
in multifactor productivity that was so important for economic growth during this period cannot be explained by the BLS.[2]

This pattern of economic growth did not continue through the 1970s.
Output per capita continued to grow, but at the slower pace of 1.2 percent
per year between 1973 and 1981. Growth in labor productivity slowed to
0.8 percent per year, and it was only because labor force participation increased substantially as the baby-boom generation came of age and more
women entered the work force that output per capita continued to increase. BLS attributes part of this decline in productivity to slower growth

---

2. Other researchers have had no better luck. See, for example, John W. Kendrick,
"The Implications of Growth Accounting Models," in Hulten and Sawhill, eds., *The Legacy
of Reaganomics*.

TABLE 17

SOURCES OF GROWTH IN PER CAPITA REAL OUTPUT, 1948-1981
(Average annual growth rate)

	1948-1981	1948-1973	1973-1981	1948-1973/ 1973-1981 Difference
Productivity (output/hr)[a]	2.4	3.0	0.8	−2.2
Due to growth in				
Capital/hr	0.9	1.0	0.7	−0.3
Multifactor productivity[b]	1.5	2.0	0.1	−1.9
(Explained)	(0.6)	(0.8)	(0.0)	(−0.8)
(Unexplained)	(0.9)	(1.2)	(0.1)	(−1.1)
Labor force as a share of				
the population[c]	0.4	0.1	1.4	1.3
Hours worked per member of				
the labor force[d]	−0.9	−0.8	−1.0	−0.2
Per capita real output	1.9	2.2	1.2	−1.0

SOURCE: BLS.
NOTE: The rate of growth of real per capita output is the sum of the rates of growth of productivity, labor force, and hours.

a. Constant-dollar gross domestic product in the private business sector per hour of all persons engaged in that sector.

b. Factors explaining multifactor productivity growth are intersectoral shifts in labor, changes in the composition of the labor force, growth of research and development, decreases in hours worked relative to hours paid, and changes in the utilization of capital.

c. Includes growth in working age population as a share of the population and increases in the labor force participation rate.

d. The BLS series used to estimate hours worked is actually a mixture of hours worked and hours paid. Consequently, to the extent that the number of hours paid for but not worked has risen since 1948, these calculations may understate the decline in the number of hours actually worked per member of the labor force. SEE: John W. Kendrick and Elliot S. Grossman, *Productivity in the United States* (Baltimore: Johns Hopkins University Press, 1980), p. 25.

in capital per worker, but most of it to the fact that multifactor productivity growth slowed from an average annual growth rate of 2 percent to 0.1 percent. Moreover, BLS is unable to explain much of the drop in multifactor productivity. Whatever had been making a major contribution to productivity growth in the earlier period ceased to do so, but we do not know what it was or where it went.

The Reagan administration blamed the growing size and intrusiveness of the federal government for the slowdown in productivity growth in the 1970s. In the remainder of this section we examine evidence on the size and intrusiveness of the federal government to see if the administration's claims can be supported.

The Size of Government

Table 18 shows that government spending at all levels grew more than one-and-one-half times faster than other spending between the 1950s and the 1970s, rising from an average of 26 percent of GNP to an average of 32 percent of GNP. Federal government expenditures increased more rapidly than federal government receipts, widening the federal budget deficit. At the same time, state and local government receipts grew faster than their expenditures, leading to growing state and local surpluses. Thus, total government receipts increased roughly in line with total government expenditures, and, as a share of GNP, the budget deficit for all levels of government combined increased only 0.8 percentage points.

Although these data show quite clearly that government has grown larger, one must be careful in moving from the observation that taxes and spending are rising as a share of GNP to the conclusion that government's ultimate claim on the nation's resources is rising. Federal, state, and local purchases of goods and services (to pay teachers, build highways, or buy weapons, for example), which do absorb resources directly, rose only 1.6 points as a share of GNP between the 1950s and the 1960s (from 19.5 to 21.1 percent of GNP) and they actually fell slightly between the 1960s and the 1970s. Meanwhile, between the 1950s and the 1970s, transfers to persons by all levels of government (Unemployment Compensation, Food Stamps, and Social Security, for example), which represent a redistribution of income among the nation's citizens but no direct absorption of resources, rose 4.8 percentage points (from 4 to 8.8). At the federal level, purchases of goods and services actually fell 3.8 percentage points as a share of GNP with the decline in the relative importance of defense expenditures, whereas transfers and interest rose 4.6 points.

In short, President Reagan was correct in his characterization of this period as one in which government showed a proclivity to tax and spend, but this characterization misses the important point that most of the growth in taxes and spending has been for transfer programs. Moreover, 80 percent of these transfers are for Social Security and other social insurance programs that serve middle-income groups and enjoy widespread political support.

Despite this growth in transfers, the United States has yet to become a welfare state by the standards of the rest of the industrialized world. Total government spending as a percentage of GNP is significantly lower in this country than it is in most other industrialized countries. Furthermore, there is no apparent relationship between the size of a country's public sector and its rate of growth. Between 1970 and 1980, among the seven largest industrial nations, only Japan had a smaller public sector than the

TABLE 18

GROWTH IN GOVERNMENT
(*Percentage of GNP by decades*)

	1950–1959	1960–1969	1970–1979
Receipts			
Federal	18.4	19.0	19.4
State and local[a]	8.1	11.1	14.9
Less: federal grants to state and local governments	−0.9	−1.7	−3.2
	25.6	28.4	31.1
Expenditures			
Federal[b]	18.2	19.3	21.3
State and local	8.4	11.0	13.9
Less: federal grants to state and local governments	−0.9	−1.7	−3.2
	25.7	28.6	32.0
Deficits			
Federal	0.1	−0.3	−1.8
State and local	−0.2	0.1	0.9
	−0.1	−0.2	−0.9
Federal debt[c]	60.1	40.2	28.2

Sources of Expenditure Growth

	1950–1959	1960–1969	1970–1979
Federal			
Purchases of goods and services	11.8	10.7	8.0
Transfers to persons	3.3	4.7	7.9
Other[d]	2.2	2.2	2.2
	17.3	17.6	18.1
State and Local			
Purchases of goods and services	7.7	10.4	13.0
Transfers and other[e]	0.7	0.6	0.9
	8.4	11.0	13.9
Addendum:			
Total government purchases of goods and services	19.5	21.1	21.0
Total government transfers	4.0	5.3	8.8

SOURCE: *Economic Report of the President* (Washington, D.C.: Government Printing Office, 1984), tables B-1, p. 220, and B-75 through B-77, pp. 308–310; Office of Management and Budget, "Federal Government Finances, 1985 Budget Data," February 1984.

a. State and local receipts include grants-in-aid from the federal government.

b. Federal expenditures include grants to state and local governments.

c. Debt held by the public as a percentage of GNP.

d. Transfers to foreigners, net interest paid, and subsidies less current surplus of government enterprises.

e. Transfers to persons, net interest paid less dividends, and subsidies less current surplus of government enterprises.

United States, yet four of the remaining five experienced a faster rate of growth.[3]

Thus, there is little evidence that the size of government itself was a key contributor to the slowing of economic growth and the decline in productivity that the Reagan administration's economic recovery program sought to reverse. Nevertheless, rising marginal tax rates, increasingly generous transfer programs, and increasingly burdensome regulations—even though they absorb few resources directly—can adversely affect growth by reducing incentives to work, save, and invest and by lowering economic efficiency. These are the effects emphasized in the supply-siders' indictment of big government; but what is the evidence of their quantitative importance in contributing to the slowdown in economic growth and productivity?

Labor Force Growth and Saving

There is little prima facie evidence to support the view that either work or saving was discouraged during the 1970s. We have already noted that there was a large increase in the labor force at the same time taxes and transfers were rising. Net private saving as a share of GNP did decline somewhat, but gross private saving actually rose a little (figure 11). More careful attempts to isolate the effects of taxes and transfers on people's behavior suggest that taxes and transfers do reduce work effort and may reduce saving, but the effects are far more modest and uncertain than supply-side rhetoric sometimes implies. (This evidence is discussed more fully later.)

Investment

The administration argues that growth in capital per worker slowed after 1973 because effective tax rates on income from capital rose during the 1970s. This happened because business taxes are levied on nominal profits, which can rise during periods of inflation even though profits adjusted for inflation are falling. When this happens, the after tax rate of return on capital falls and investment is discouraged.[4]

Once again, this view has merit, but its importance may have been exaggerated. First, recent research indicates that effective tax rates on in-

---

3. Mancur Olson, "Ideology and Economic Growth," in Hulten and Sawhill, eds., *The Legacy of Reaganomics*; Congressional Budget Office, *Balancing the Federal Budget and Limiting Federal Spending: Constitutional and Statutory Approaches* (Washington, D.C.: Government Printing Office, September 1982), pp. 16–22.

4. See, for example, *Economic Report of the President*, (Washington, D.C.: Government Printing Office, 1983) p. 92.

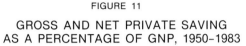

FIGURE 11

GROSS AND NET PRIVATE SAVING
AS A PERCENTAGE OF GNP, 1950–1983

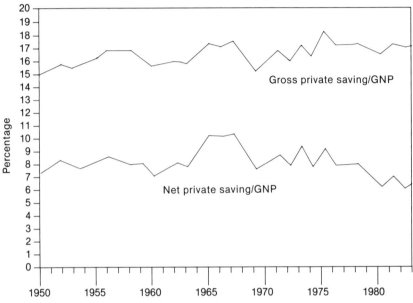

SOURCE: U.S. Department of Commerce, BEA.

come from capital are less sensitive to the rate of inflation than we once thought[5] and that, if anything, there was a slight decrease in effective tax rates on capital during the 1970s (table 19). Second, investment as a share of GNP was no lower in the 1970s than it was during the earlier post-World War II period. The slower growth in the amount of capital per worker that occurred during the 1970s was due to the dramatic expansion of the labor force, not to less investment. Finally, if the tax rate on capital were in fact rising, the pretax return on investment would be expected to rise, but a recent estimate shows it falling from 11 percent in 1967 to 8 percent in 1980 on a cyclically adjusted basis.[6]

To conclude that government policies did not discourage capital formation in the 1970s compared with earlier periods is not, however, to say

---

5. Don Fullerton and Yolanda K. Henderson, "Incentive Effects of Taxes on Income from Capital: Alternative Policies in the 1980s," in Hulten and Sawhill, eds., *The Legacy of Reaganomics*.

6. Barry P. Bosworth, "Capital Formation, Technology, and Economic Policy," *Brookings Papers on Economic Activity*, 1982:2, pp. 273–326.

TABLE 19

Trends in Effective Tax Rates and in Nonresidential Fixed Investment
as a Percentage of GNP and NNP, 1950-1982

Period	Effective Tax Rates[a]	Gross I/GNP[b]	Net I/NNP[c]
1950-1982	35.8[d]	10.2	3.3
1950-1959	54.7[d]	9.6	3.1
1960-1969	39.9	10.0	3.6
1970-1979	34.4	10.7	3.4
1970	52.3	10.5	3.7
1971	31.3	10.0	3.2
1972	31.3	10.2	3.4
1973	34.1	10.8	4.3
1974	39.3	10.9	3.8
1975	32.1	10.2	2.2
1976	31.4	10.1	2.2
1977	30.6	10.7	2.9
1978	31.4	11.5	3.8
1979	30.0	12.0	3.1
1980-1982	14.2	11.7	3.0
1980	33.1	11.7	3.3
1981	4.7	11.9	3.4
1982	15.8	11.3	2.2

Sources: Charles R. Hulten and James W. Robertson, "The Taxation of High Technology
Industries," Changing Domestic Priorities Discussion Paper (Washington, D.C.:
The Urban Institute, September 1983), p. 7. Rates for 1981 and 1982 assume a 4
percent real rate of return and a 6 percent expected rate of inflation; U.S. Department of Commerce, BEA.

    a. Marginal effective corporate tax rate on new plant and equipment.

    b. Gross private, nonresidential, fixed investment as a percentage of GNP.

    c. Net private, nonresidential, fixed investment as a percentage of Net National Product
(NNP).

    d. 1952-1982 and 1952-1959 averages respectively.

there was no problem. Given the large increase in labor force participation
during the 1970s, more capital formation would have been needed simply
to maintain past rates of growth in capital per worker and productivity.
Furthermore, some analysts have suggested that much of the capital stock
was made less valuable by the sharp increase in energy prices after 1973
and that a higher rate of capital formation would have been necessary simply to restore the effective capital stock to earlier levels.[7] Finally, given the

---

    7. Martin Neil Baily, "Productivity and the Services of Capital and Labor," Brookings
Papers on Economic Activity, 1981:1, pp. 1-50; Ernst R. Berndt and David O. Wood, "Engi-
neering and Econometric Interpretations of Energy Capital Complementarity," American
Economic Review, vol. 69, no. 3 (June 1979), pp. 342-354.

large proportion of the decline in productivity that remains unexplained, capital formation takes on greater importance as one of the few things that policy can influence in order to stimulate greater productivity.

Regulation

Experts attribute between 10 and 25 percent of the productivity slowdown to the growth of social regulation during the 1970s.[8] As the scope of environmental, health, safety, and consumer protection regulation expanded, businesses were forced to spend money on compliance that could otherwise have gone to producing more goods and services. Although there are obvious benefits from cleaner air, safer products, and a healthier workplace, these benefits do not usually show up in conventional measures of output such as the GNP. Thus, even when measured productivity growth falls, social welfare more broadly conceived can improve. Of course, in cases where regulations are badly designed, the output foregone in complying with the regulations will be higher than necessary. In such cases, reform rather than elimination of the offending rules is an obvious solution. Beyond this, scaling back regulations entails clear-cut social costs, and the choice between more material growth and, say, a cleaner, safer environment is a matter over which people can disagree. The Reagan administration has apparently come down largely on the side of greater material growth.

All in all, the Reagan administration properly focused on slower productivity growth as a major cause of the disappointing growth in living standards during the 1970s; but it probably placed too much blame on past government policies as the cause of the problem and thus too much hope in its own policies as the solution. However, a closer look at the evidence on how the economy performed between 1981 and 1983 and at the likely long-term effects of the administration's policies is warranted.

Supply-Side Effects in the Short Run

The Reagan administration originally promised immediate results from its supply-side program. The economy's poor performance during the 1981–1982 recession enabled its critics to label the program a failure. Supporters, conversely, point to the recovery as evidence that the program is

---

8. For a review of the literature, see Gregory B. Christainsen and Robert H. Haveman, "The Reagan Administration's Regulatory Relief Effort and Productivity," in George C. Eads and Michael Fix, eds., *The Reagan Regulatory Strategy: An Assessment* (Washington, D.C.: The Urban Institute Press, 1984).

now working. Neither view is correct. Supply-side economic indicators such as investment and productivity growth normally decline during a recession and can be expected to grow strongly during recovery. But a lower-than-normal decline or faster-than-normal rebound in these indicators would at least be encouraging signs. How have they performed over the most recent business cycle compared with their performance in previous cycles?

The story told in figure 12 is that, by and large, there has been no discernible supply-side response to date.[9] As measured by the decline in real GNP, the recession was quite severe by historical standards. The rebound in real output throughout the first year of the most recent recovery was quite typical, but its second-year performance may turn out to be unusually strong. Given the severity of the downturn, the precipitous decline in investment was not unexpected. Gross business saving (depreciation allowances and corporate retained earnings), in contrast, exhibited a strikingly unusual pattern in comparison with the average pattern in previous downturns, increasing as a percentage of GNP rather than decreasing over the course of the recession. The buoyancy of business saving in the face of recession was partially attributable to the 1981–1982 changes in the tax laws governing depreciation. Of course, more business saving in and of itself was not the intended effect of the business tax cuts. To improve the rate of capital formation, such saving must be reinvested. The rebound in investment during the recovery was much faster than normal, but this strong rebound has merely recovered most of the above-average losses in investment during the downturn (note the change over the entire cycle recorded in figure 12).

Like business saving, personal saving also behaved atypically during the most recent cycle. Personal saving (as a percentage of GNP) declined over the course of the recession and into the first half of the recovery, hitting its lowest level in thirty-three years in the second quarter of 1983.[10] The special tax incentives meant to encourage greater personal saving

---

9. Although useful, these comparisons should be interpreted with care for three reasons: (1) They are not adjusted for the greater severity of the most recent recession. (2) They are complicated by the incomplete recovery from the 1980 recession that serves as the base for measuring the path of each indicator during the 1981–1982 recession. (3) Factors other than the Reagan administration's policies could cause these indicators to behave differently during the most recent recession and recovery period. See table 20 and the accompanying discussion for an attempt to correct some of these problems.

10. The following explanations have been offered for the decline in personal saving: Two back-to-back recessions and the unexpected severity of the most recent recession caused consumers to deplete their savings; consumption increased in anticipation of the final 10 percent cut in tax rates; the combination of the drop in inflation and the surge in stock values increases consumers' net worth; the baby-boom generation has reached the age at which consumption propensities are high.

FIGURE 12

SUPPLY-SIDE INDICATORS DURING RECESSION AND RECOVERY

Recession	Recovery
6 quarters prior to trough	Trough (T) = 100
(T − 6) = 100	

REAL GNP

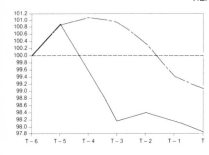 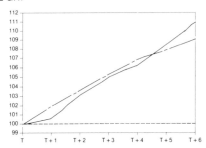

Change from T − 6 to T + 6:
Average of 5 previous cycles · · · + 7.95
1981–1984 cycle · · · · · · · · · · · · · + 8.44

BUSINESS FIXED INVESTMENT AS A PERCENTAGE OF GNP

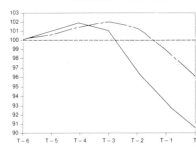 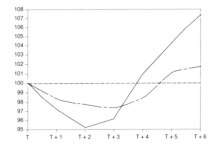

Change from T − 6 to T + 6:
Average of 5 previous cycles · · · − 2.16
1981–1984 cycle · · · · · · · · · · · · · − 2.71

— — —— average of 5 previous cycles[a]
———— 1981–1984 cycle

FIGURE 12 (Continued)

SUPPLY-SIDE INDICATORS DURING RECESSION AND RECOVERY

Recession	Recovery
6 quarters prior to trough	Trough (T) = 100
(T − 6) = 100	

BUSINESS SAVING AS A PERCENTAGE OF GNP

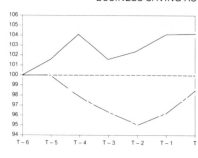 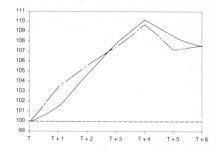

Change from T − 6 to T + 6:
Average of 5 previous cycles ••• + 5.85
1981–1984 cycle ••••••••••• + 11.68

PERSONAL SAVINGS AS A PERCENTAGE OF GNP

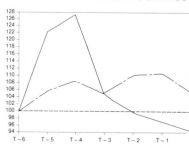 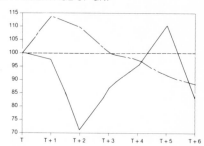

Change from T − 6 to T + 6:
Average of 5 previous cycles ••• − 6.64
1981–1984 cycle ••••••••••• − 21.08

— — — — — average of 5 previous cycles[a]
——————— 1981–1984 cycle

FIGURE 12 (Continued)

SUPPLY-SIDE INDICATORS DURING RECESSION AND RECOVERY

Recession
6 quarters prior to trough
(T − 6) = 100

Recovery
Trough (T) = 100

OUTPUT PER HOUR (NONFARM BUSINESS SECTOR)

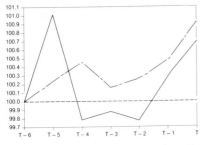 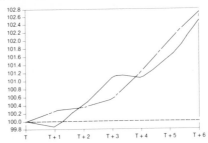

Change from T − 6 to T + 6:
Average of 5 previous cycles .. + 5.68
1981–1984 cycle .... + 4.59

CIVILIAN LABOR FORCE

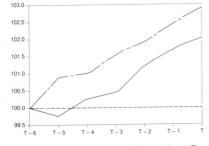 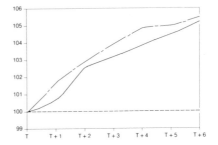

Change from T − 6 to T + 6:
Average of 5 previous cycles ... + 6.37
1981–1984 cycle .... + 5.90

—— — —— average of 5 previous cycles[a]
————— 1981–1984 cycle

SOURCES: Constructed from data published by the U.S. Department of Commerce, BEA, and
by the U.S. Department of Labor, BLS.
a. Averages based on six quarters preceding and following these business cycle
troughs (as designated by the National Bureau of Economic Research): 1954 II, 1958 II, 1961 I,
1970 IV, 1975 I. The 1948–1950 cycle (trough: 1949 IV) was excluded because the outbreak of
the Korean War in 1950 distorted the strength of the recovery. The 1979–1981 cycle (trough:
1980 III) was excluded because the recovery lasted only half as long as any other recovery of
the post-World War II era.

turned out to be poorly designed for that purpose.[11] For example, a study of the impact of the increased availability of IRAs on personal saving during 1982 indicates that most of the increase in IRA contributions during the year reflected a shift of funds into IRAs out of other assets, not an increase in saving.[12] In the future, once such transfers have been exhausted, these tax incentives could induce greater saving.

In the initial stages of recovery, productivity normally registers sharp increases, as employers boost output without adding new workers to their payrolls. As the recovery continues and employers become convinced that it will be sustained, new workers are hired and the growth in productivity slows. The growth in productivity thus far into the recovery, however, has not shown a stronger increase than in previous upturns. The prospects for a stronger rate of productivity growth over the longer term are discussed at the end of this chapter.

The growth in the labor force leveled off during the second half of 1983 in contrast to the more sustained growth in previous recovery periods. In fact, it is the slow growth in the labor force, not a larger-than-normal increase in employment, that accounted for the dramatic decline in the unemployment rate over this period.[13] Explanations for this labor force slowdown fall into two categories: (1) there were large numbers of "discouraged workers," and (2) the baby-boom generation is aging and the flood of new women workers into the labor force has slowed. Both appear to have contributed to the slowdown.

Another way to assess whether there has been any short-run supply-side response to the president's program is to examine the extent to which existing models of saving, investment, and labor supply have accurately predicted these variables since 1981. Because most of the large-scale macroeconomic forecasting models do not include supply-side influences, or do so in only a limited way, a finding that they have underpredicted these variables since 1981 would suggest that such influences were beginning to play a role.

In an analysis of the results from three macroeconomic models (table 20), Alan Blinder finds that personal saving has been lower than the

11. See Harvey Galper and Eugene Steurle, "The Design of Tax Incentives to Encourage Savings," Brookings Discussion Papers in Economics (Washington, D.C.: The Brookings Institution, 1983).

12. See Robin C. De Magistris and Carl J. Palash, "Impact of IRAs on Saving," *Federal Reserve Bank of New York Quarterly Review*, vol. 7, no. 4 (Winter 1982-83), pp. 24-32.

13. Peter Duprey, "The Surprising Drop in Unemployment," *Review of the U.S. Economy, January 1984* (Lexington, Mass.: Data Resources, Inc.), pp. 1.19-1.21).

TABLE 20

EVIDENCE OF A SUPPLY-SIDE RESPONSE IN THREE MACROECONOMIC
MODELS, 1981–1983

	Labor Supply	Personal Saving	Business Fixed Investment
Data Resources, Inc., quarterly model	No	No	Yes
Wharton Econometric Forecasting Associates, Inc., annual model	Yes	No	Yes
Massachusetts Institute of Technology–University of Pennsylvania–Social Science Research Council quarterly model	Yes	No	Yes

SOURCE: Adapted from Alan S. Blinder, "The Message in the Models," in Charles R. Hulten and Isabel V. Sawhill, eds., *The Legacy of Reaganomics: Prospects for Long-Term Growth* (Washington, D.C.: The Urban Institute Press, 1984).

NOTE: "No" means the model overpredicted the variable.

"Yes" means the model underpredicted the variable.

models were predicting and investment higher.[14] The results for labor force participation are mixed. Based on this evidence, we could conclude that investment, at least, has been favorably affected by the business tax cuts.

Supply-Side Effects in the Long Run

No one should have expected the administration's supply-side program to have had much, if any, impact during a period when the economy was depressed. But once the economy has fully recovered from the recession and is operating at a high level of resource utilization, the administration's tax, spending, and regulatory initiatives may well have some more positive effects.

In examining the likely magnitude of these effects, it is important to understand two points at the outset. First, most supply-side policies have

14. Because the personal and business tax cuts have been phased in gradually, another possibility is that people will save, invest, and work less now in anticipation of greater gains once the policies are fully implemented. It is these expectational effects that Alan S. Blinder investigated, not the short-run supply-side responses that we emphasize here. See Blinder, "The Message in the Models," in Hulten and Sawhill, eds., *The Legacy of Reaganomics*.

only a temporary effect on the economy's growth rate. A reduction in taxes or regulatory burdens prompts a one-time adjustment in the amount of capital formation, saving, or work that people want to do. During the period of adjustment, the rate of growth accelerates, but after a few years it returns to its former path, albeit at a level of output higher than before (figure 13). To permanently affect the rate of growth, it would be necessary to continuously lower taxes or pare back regulations, an obvious impossibility. Alternatively, the pace of technological change could be increased, but this is a process that is poorly understood and probably not easily influenced. Second, as the label "supply-side" implies, these policies primarily affect the economy's *capacity* to produce goods and services. If there is insufficient demand to fully employ the existing labor force and capital plant, additions to this supply will have little or no effect on the economy's observed growth rate.[15] But as the economy recovers and total spending rises, the availability of a larger labor force or an expanded capital stock can help prevent a resurgence of inflation and enable the economy to achieve a higher level of real output at the next peak in the business cycle. Have the Reagan administration's policies been well designed to achieve this outcome?

Capital Formation

The overall impact of the Reagan administration's policies on capital formation depends on a number of factors: the excess capacity created during the recession, the business tax cuts, the reduced federal outlays on capital goods, the greater tax incentives for private saving, and the higher deficits (table 21). The business tax cuts are likely to have positive effects, but these will be offset, at least to some extent, by the discouraging effect of excess industrial capacity during the first half of the decade and by the federal budget deficits' absorption of saving during the second half of the decade. What one concludes about the effect of Reagan policies on public investment depends on one's assumptions about how productive such investments have been.

The Reagan administration's tax cuts for business were designed to increase the overall rate of private investment. Even if a tight monetary policy were to raise interest rates and thereby discourage investment generally, these tax cuts would at least encourage a shift of resources from hous-

---

15. Greater incentives for investment do affect demand as well as supply because spending for capital goods employs resources and generates income in the same way that spending for consumer goods does.

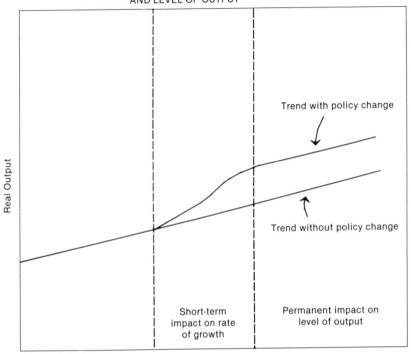

FIGURE 13

HOW SUPPLY-SIDE POLICIES AFFECT THE RATE OF GROWTH
AND LEVEL OF OUTPUT

Real Output

Trend with policy change

Trend without policy change

Short-term
impact on rate
of growth

Permanent impact on
level of output

Time

ing and consumer durables to spending on plant and equipment. This focus on changing the mix as well as the level of investment spending has
been dubbed the "Feldstein twist," after the former chairman of the President's Council of Economic Advisers, who initially advanced the idea to
justify combining a tight monetary policy with a stimulative, but targeted,
fiscal policy.

Overall, the effective tax rate on income from capital fell from 26.4
percent to 22.8 percent—14 percent—as a result of the provisions of the
1981 and 1982 tax acts.[16] This average conceals much diversity in the treatment of different types of assets. Most important, it combines a sharp drop
of 52 percent in the rates that apply to returns on new investment in plant
and equipment with no change in the tax treatment of other types of capital, such as inventories, land, and owner-occupied housing.

---

16. Fullerton and Henderson, "Incentive Effects of Taxes on Income from Capital," in
Hulten and Sawhill, eds., *The Legacy of Reaganomics.*

TABLE 21

Estimated Impact of the Reagan Administration's Policies on
Capital Formation

	Percentage Change in the Stock of Capital during the 1980s	
	Lower Bound	Upper Bound
Investment (Demand for capital)		
Recession[a]	−2.5	−1
Tax incentives for private investment[b]	+2	+4
Public investment[c]	−3	+1
Saving (Supply of capital)		
Tax incentives for private saving[d]	0	+3
Deficits[e]	−6	−3

Source: Authors' calculations.

a. Based on a comparison of the ratio of residential and nonresidential investment to GNP in the simulations of actual policies and the alternative policies that moderate the recession discussed in chapter 3. The results of this exercise suggest that the ratio of net investment to GNP is reduced by about 1.5 percent for three to five years as the result of the excessive slack engendered by the recession. The impacts on the stock of capital and GNP are estimated using the simulation model described in appendix B.

b. Assumes that the cost of capital falls by about 3 percent as the result of the tax legislation in 1981 and 1982 and that drop increases the stock of capital by an equivalent amount. See Don Fullerton and Yolanda K. Henderson, "Incentive Effects of Taxes on Income from Capital: Alternative Policies in the 1980s," in Hulten and Sawhill, eds., *The Legacy of Reaganomics*; Stephen Oliner, Robert Haveman, and Martin David, "Investment in Equipment, Structures, and Research Capital Under the Reagan Tax Acts," unpublished manuscript, University of Wisconsin—Madison, March 1983. Note that this is an estimate for all types of capital. The increased demand for business capital, especially structures, is predicted to be greater.

c. According to Charles L. Schultze, real federal spending on physical investment (both direct and grants-in-aid) declined from $14.0 billion in 1981 to $12.1 billion (estimated) in 1984—13.5 percent. Including just "growth-oriented" expenditures, there was an increase from $7.3 billion to $7.7 billion—5.5 percent. The stock of government-owned fixed capital represents about 25 percent of the total stock according to BEA (Survey of Current Business, August 1983), so the estimated percentage changes in the total stock are between minus 3 percent and plus 1 percent. Because these figures exclude direct spending by state and local governments and because the prior trend in spending for public capital had been positive, if anything, these estimates probably understate the impact of Reagan policies. See Donald A. Nichols, "Federal Spending Priorities and Long-Term Economic Growth" and Charles L. Schultze, "Alternate Measures of Federal Investment Outlays," in Hulten and Sawhill, eds., *The Legacy of Reaganomics*.

d. Assumes a net tax decrease of 10 percent attributable to Reagan, increasing the after-tax rate of return to savings by 7 percent, and savings itself by 0 to 4 percent for every 10 percent increase in rate of return. See Michael J. Boskin, "Taxation, Saving, and the Rate of Interest," *Journal of Political Economy*, vol. 86, no. 2, part 2 (April 1978), pp. S3–S27; E. Philip Howrey and Saul H. Hymans, "The Measurement and Determination of Loanable-Funds Savings," *Brookings Papers on Economic Activity*, 1978, vol. 3, pp. 655–685; and Herbert Stein and Murray Foss, "Taxes and Saving," *AEI Economist*, July 1981.

e. Lower bound assumes that deficits reduce net savings as a percentage of GNP by two percentage points. Upper bound assumes a reduction of one percentage point. See appendix B for a description of the model used to generate the impact on the stock of capital.

By itself, this drop in tax rates could be expected to reduce the overall cost of capital (of which taxes are only one component) by about 3 percent and to increase the amount of capital that businesses find it profitable to acquire by perhaps 3 percent.

The Effects of the Recession

Offsetting these positive effects of lower taxes on the incentive to invest in the future is the discouraging effect that the 1981–1982 recession had on the accumulation of capital. We estimate that the recession has reduced the capital stock by between 1 and 2.5 percent relative to what it would now be if capacity utilization rates had not been so severely depressed in the early 1980s (table 21).

The Availability of Saving

Once the economy is operating closer to capacity, the rate of capital formation will depend more on the availability of saving than on incentives to invest. Here, the administration has taken two actions with potentially contradictory effects. On the one hand, it has put in place some incentives to encourage greater private saving. On the other, it has created large future claims against this saving by increasing the size of the deficit.

Several provisions of the Economic Recovery Tax Act (ERTA) of 1981—the reduction in marginal tax rates on personal income and the increased availability of individual retirement accounts (IRAs), for example—were directed toward encouraging greater personal saving.[17] At first glance, the premise underlying these provisions—that an improvement in the rate of return to saving (via reduced taxation) will induce people to save more—seems to make sense. Economic research, however, has yet to provide evidence to unequivocally support that premise. Although the most recent research points toward a positive relationship, an optimistic estimate is that a 10 percent increase in the rate of return might induce a 4 percent increase in saving.[18] Other estimates predict no significant impact.[19] On the basis of this evidence, and the fact that the Reagan administration's policies have increased the after-tax rate of return by about 7 per-

---

17. Other ERTA provisions designed to increase personal saving include the reduction in the marginal tax rate on high income taxpayers from 70 to 50 percent; the interest exclusion provision scheduled for 1985 (eliminated as part of the "downpayment" on the deficit in 1984); and the reduction in the top marginal rate on capital gains from 28 to 20 percent. See *Economic Report of the President, 1983*, pp. 87–89.

18. Michael J. Boskin, "Taxation, Saving, and the Rate of Interest," *Journal of Political Economy*, vol. 86, no. 2, part 2 (April 1978), pp. S3–S27.

19. E. Philip Howrey and Saul H. Hymans, "The Measurement and Determination of Loanable-Funds Saving," *Brookings Papers on Economic Activity*, 1978, vol. 3, pp. 655–685.

cent,[20] we estimate an increase in capital formation of between 0 and 3 percent from this source.

The Effect of Budget Deficits

For the 1976–1980 period, deficits averaged 2 percent of GNP. For the 1984–1989 period they are projected to be $1.3 trillion, reaching 5 to 6 percent of GNP by the end of the decade. For this reason alone, then, the net saving available to the private sector could decline by as much as three or four percentage points. Of course, some corrective measures will undoubtedly be taken to reduce these "out-year" deficits. Moreover, whatever deficits remain may be partially offset by a rise in state and local surpluses, by some additional private saving, and by inflows of foreign capital. (In addition to the specific tax incentives mentioned earlier, greater saving could be induced by higher interest rates.) Another possibility is that households will save more in anticipation of having to pay higher taxes later to reduce the national debt. Some economists predict that these offsets will be quite large. Lawrence Summers estimates that an extra dollar of deficit will increase private saving by about thirty cents, foreign saving by about twenty-five cents, and state and local surpluses by about five cents.[21] Others find little reason to expect offsets of this magnitude.[22] The overall saving rate has never shown much variation in response to changed economic conditions. State and local governments are likely to reduce taxes or increase expenditures rather than allow larger surpluses to accumulate. And substantial capital inflows from abroad, while currently very large, may be neither sustainable nor desirable.

Given these uncertainties, it is hard to estimate the impact of the deficits with much confidence. In table 21, we assume they will reduce the net

---

20. This figure assumes that there would have been some reduction in taxes to offset bracket creep even if Reagan had not been elected. A 10 percent tax cut represents the amount by which the Reagan administration's personal tax cuts exceed the cuts under an indexed system. A 10 percent reduction in taxes would increase the after-tax rate of return on savings by about 7 percent. (The pre-Reagan-administration marginal tax rate on income from capital averaged 40 percent; this rate drops to 36 percent and the after-tax rate of return increases from 60 to 64 percent of the pre-tax rate, a 6.7 percent increase. Hence the 6.7 percent figure.) For a similar analysis and excellent review of the literature on saving, see Herbert Stein and Murray Foss, "Taxes and Saving," *AEI Economist*, July 1981, p. 6. They calculate the effects of the full 25 percent reduction in tax rates rather than assuming that there would have been some reduction to offset bracket creep even if Reagan had not been elected.

21. Summers, "The Legacy of Current Macroeconomic Policies," in Hulten and Sawhill, eds., *The Legacy of Reaganomics*.

22. See, for example, Benjamin M. Friedman, "Implications of the Government Deficit for U.S. Capital Formation," in Federal Reserve Bank of Boston, Proceedings of a Conference held in October 1983 at Melvin Village, New Hampshire, *The Conference Series*, No. 27 (October 1983).

investment ratio by one to two percentage points during the 1980s. Under these assumptions, which are reasonably conservative, their negative effects on capital formation still stand out clearly and roughly cancel any positive effects from the supply-side tax cuts.[23] The Feldstein twist shifts much of the burden onto residential investment, but business investment also is adversely affected (table 11). What this analysis also makes clear is that reducing the out-year deficits would be a big plus for growth. To the extent that deficits can be eliminated without reversing the supply-side incentives introduced in 1981, that would be better still. Broadening the tax base, for example, would be preferable to raising marginal rates or taxing income from capital more heavily.

Public Investment

This diversion of resources into the public sector would not necessarily be bad for growth if a substantial portion of these resources were being used for public investment purposes and if such projects carried a rate of return at least as high as the rate for such projects in the private sector, but that is not the case. With the exception of the highway program enacted in late 1982 largely in reaction to congressional concern about high unemployment, spending for capital improvements has tended to decline under the Reagan administration. Moreover, although popular rhetoric would suggest otherwise, rates of return to infrastructure investments appear to be quite low,[24] and the Reagan administration appears to have cut most deeply the projects with the smallest payoffs. If these resources are then made available for more productive private investment, the "effective" capital stock might actually increase.[25]

To summarize, we conclude, first, that there will be some net stimulus to investment from the Reagan administration's tax program. If large defi-

---

23. Deficits might not affect personal standards of living until well into the future. Consumption initially rises as larger deficits increase aggregate demand. Consumption is lowered after perhaps ten to twenty-five years, as the lower saving implied by the initial "consumption binge" slows capital formation and, ultimately, output. See Edward M. Gramlich, "How Bad Are The Large Deficits?" in Gregory B. Mills and John L. Palmer, eds., *Federal Budget Policy in the 1980s* (Washington, D.C.: The Urban Institute Press, 1984).

24. Donald A. Nichols, "Federal Spending Priorities and Long-Term Economic Growth," in Hulten and Sawhill, eds., *The Legacy of Reaganomics*; Kiran Bhatt, Ronald Kirby, and Michael Beesly, "The Federal Role in Infrastructure Renewal," Changing Domestic Priorities Discussion Paper (Washington, D.C.: The Urban Institute, December 1983).

25. Charles L. Schultze, "Alternative Measures of Federal Investment Outlays," in Hulten and Sawhill, eds., *The Legacy of Reaganomics*. Schultze shows that there has been no decline in what he calls "growth-oriented" expenditures on physical investment as a percentage of GNP under the Reagan administration although there has been a decline in total expenditures for this purpose.

cits end up absorbing much of the saving needed to finance this investment, however, growth will, on balance, be adversely affected. Second, because the tax incentives have been targeted on business investment, the mix of investment spending is likely to change even if the total should be somewhat smaller. Investment in plant and equipment will be less affected than investment in housing and consumer durables.[26] This shift in priorities will be welcome by people who feel we are a housing-rich nation, but younger families may find it more difficult to acquire their own homes during the 1980s.

The Labor Force

During the decade of the 1970s, the civilian labor force grew very rapidly. Recessions tended to slow but not reverse the upward trend and, as we have seen, the 1981–1982 downturn was no exception (figure 12). For a variety of demographic reasons, the growth of the labor force is not predicted to be as rapid in the coming decade as it was in the last. But the Reagan administration's tax cuts, together with the reduced availability or generosity of income transfers, can be expected to induce greater work effort (more labor force participation or longer hours) and to raise the size of the full-time-equivalent labor force above what it otherwise would have been. These changes may also encourage people to choose more entrepreneurial, difficult, or unpleasant types of work than they have chosen in the past because the net financial rewards for doing so have been increased.[27]

Estimates of the responsiveness of labor supply to taxes and transfers vary, but a careful review of the available evidence by Robert Haveman, summarized in table 22, suggests that the labor force might increase by anywhere from 0.8 percent to 2.5 percent as a result of the Reagan administration's changes. Most estimates have tended to cluster around the lower of these two figures.[28] John Kendrick, for example, argues that labor force growth will rise about 0.1 percent a year between 1981 and 1990

---

26. Simulations with large-scale macroeconomic models suggest that by 1987 the business capital stock will be higher and the housing stock lower than they would have been in the absence of the Reagan administration's program (Blinder, "The Message in the Models," in Hulten and Sawhill, eds., *The Legacy of Reaganomics*, table 4). Higher domestic investment in plant and equipment is also partially financed by an inflow of foreign capital attracted by high interest rates. But this inflow strengthens the value of the dollar, adversely affecting export- and import-competing industries.

27. Compare with the discussion in Summers, "The Legacy of Current Macroeconomic Policies," in Hulten and Sawhill, eds., *The Legacy of Reaganomics*.

28. The high estimate is based on research by Jerry A. Hausman, "Labor Supply," in Henry J. Aaron and Joseph A. Pechman, eds., *How Taxes Affect Economic Behavior* (Washington, D.C.: The Brookings Institution, 1981).

TABLE 22

ESTIMATED IMPACT OF THE REAGAN ADMINISTRATION'S POLICIES ON THE
SIZE OF THE LABOR FORCE

	Percentage Change in Full-Time Equivalents in the Labor Force during the 1980s	
	Lower Bound	*Upper Bound*
Impact due to changes in personal tax rates[a]	0.7	1.6
Impact due to changes in benefit programs[b]	0.1	0.9
Total	0.8	2.5

SOURCE: Robert Haveman, "How Much Have the Reagan Administration's Tax and Spending Policies Increased Work Effort?" in Hulten and Sawhill, eds., *The Legacy of Reaganomics*.

   a. Effects of the Economic Recovery Tax Act (ERTA) relative to an indexed personal tax system beginning in October 1981.

   b. Includes estimated effects of changes in the provisions and outlays for twenty-two different income transfer, health, education, employment, training, and social service programs. The impact of the Reagan administration's human resources and personal tax policy changes enacted between 1981 and 1983 is estimated as if they had been in effect in 1980.

(from 1.4 to 1.5 percent per year), hence, it will eventually be about 1 percent higher as a result of recent policy changes.[29]

Haveman's analysis suggests that two-thirds or more of any effect will be the result of the reduction in marginal tax rates. This finding should not be surprising because almost everyone has benefited from these cuts, and past research suggests that taxes have a significant effect on the propensity to work, especially among elderly people and married women. The rest of the estimated effect on the labor force is due to changes in benefit programs, such as Social Security, Unemployment Insurance, AFDC, and Food Stamps. Although there has been an increase in the implicit tax rates associated with many of these programs, which reduces incentives to work, basic benefits also have been cut, or, in some cases, eliminated; hence, people must work more to replace the loss of government assistance. Thus, the net effect on work effort is positive.[30]

To arrive at an overall evaluation of the Reagan program's impact on growth, we use Haveman's estimates to project an increase of 0.8 percent

---

29. Kendrick, "The Implications of Growth Accounting Models," in Hulten and Sawhill, eds., *The Legacy of Reaganomics*.

30. A large part of the impact is estimated to come as the result of more employment among workers applying for, or receiving, disability benefits. Haveman estimates that, under the Reagan administration's policies, 200,000 people a year will be denied benefits that they would have been eligible to receive under pre-Reagan-administration policies, and that about half of these people will return to the work force as a result.

to 2.5 percent in the size of the full-time labor force by 1990.[31] Like most of the numbers in this section, this is a best-guess estimate and not a precise measure of the eventual impact of the program.

Productivity

As we have seen, the growth of labor productivity is the single most important reason for rising standards of living. Economists have tended to emphasize three sources of this growth (in addition to a rise in the capital-labor ratio): a reallocation of resources from less productive to more productive uses (allocational efficiency), improvements in the quality of the labor force due to greater education and training, and advances in knowledge.[32]

Improvements in allocational efficiency occur when resources flow from sectors or activities where their marginal contribution to output is low to sectors or activities where it is higher. For many years, for example, there has been a surplus of labor in farming, so that the exodus of people from this sector has improved productivity. Most recently the concern has centered on the diversion of resources away from economically productive activities toward compliance with a proliferation of environmental, health, safety, and other social regulations. When properly designed, greater social regulations improve overall welfare but at the expense of a temporary decline in measured productivity growth. Conversely, relieving businesses of the burden of complying with such regulations, or slowing a prior trend toward more and more regulation, has a positive impact on the growth of productivity. Estimates of the impact of the Reagan administration's regulatory policies suggest that they may have increased the annual rate of measured productivity growth by as much as 0.2 percentage points above what the rate would have been if the level of regulatory activity that prevailed in the mid-1970s had continued (table 23).[33]

---

31. Most of the effects on the labor force would probably occur well before 1990, but, given continued slack in the labor market, the adjustment to these new incentives might be delayed.

32. If we use the terms from table 17, these three variables affect "multifactor productivity" while changes in the capital-labor ratio affect output per hour, or "labor productivity." This discussion leaves out changes in the quality of natural resources, economies of scale, and some other minor factors not susceptible to policy manipulation. It also ignores capacity utilization effects since we are interested here in what happens to potential GNP.

33. Kendrick, "The Implications of Growth Accounting Models," in Hulten and Sawhill, eds., *The Legacy of Reaganomics*; Christainsen and Haveman, "The Reagan Administration's Regulatory Relief Effort and Productivity," in Eads and Fix, eds., *The Reagan Regulatory Strategy: An Assessment*. Christainsen and Haveman's best guess is 0.1 relative to the 1980 level of regulatory intensity, with a range of 0 to 0.2. Kendrick's estimate is 0.2 relative to 1973–1980. For an expanded discussion of the economic impacts of the Reagan administration's regulatory program, see George C. Eads and Michael Fix, *Relief or Reform? Reagan's Regulatory Dilemma* (Washington, D.C.: The Urban Institute Press, 1984).

With respect to the quality of the labor force, the administration has reduced real outlays for education and training about 37 percent below their prior levels.[34] In the past, some portion of these outlays has simply substituted for private expenditures or for state and local spending for the same activities with no net impact on the level of human resource investments. Moreover, the rate of return on whatever additional education or training has taken place is difficult to estimate. On the basis of several reviews of the literature in this area, and of our own monitoring of the extent to which state and local governments have been replacing lost federal funds, we assume that replacement rates for federal spending could be as low as 25 percent or as high as 75 percent and that rates of return on these expenditures range between 5 and 10 percent.[35] Much of any effect will not show up soon because prospective workers who are now in elementary school will not enter the labor force until the 1990s, but in table 23 we have included a rough estimate of the likely effects over the rest of this decade.

Finally, the most important source of productivity growth is technological change. The government's role in encouraging technological advances is limited to providing a legal environment that will create appropriate incentives for private activity (through, for example, patent laws and permitting joint research and development—R&D—ventures under the antitrust laws) and to undertaking or subsidizing basic research. Because estimated rates of return on R&D investments are much higher than rates of return on tangible investments, many economists view R&D investments as a critical policy lever.[36]

Total R&D spending as a percentage of GNP reached a low of 2.2 percent in the late 1970s but is now rising and is expected to reach 2.7 percent in 1984.[37] The possible contribution of the Reagan administra-

---

34. See Congressional Budget Office, Human Resources and Community Development Division and Human Resources Cost Estimates Unit of the Budget Analysis Division, "Major Legislative Changes in Human Resources Programs Since January 1981," Staff Memorandum, August 1983. Daniel H. Saks, "Human Resource Consequences of Reagan's Social Policy," Changing Domestic Priorities Discussion Paper (Washington, D.C.: The Urban Institute, 1983).

35. Nichols, "Federal Spending Priorities and Long-Term Economic Growth," in Hulten and Sawhill, eds. *The Legacy of Reaganomics*. There is enormous variability across programs in replacement rates and rates of return. Replacement rates, for example, appear to be very high in spending for higher education and much lower in spending for compensatory education at the elementary school level and in training programs for disadvantaged workers. Rates of return are estimated to be reasonably high for such programs as the Job Corps and compensatory education but quite low or nonexistent in the case of short-term, subsidized employment programs. We have benefited from discussions with June O'Neill, Demetra Nightingale, and Margaret Simms on these issues.

36. See Barry P. Bosworth, "Capital Formation, Technology, and Economic Policy," Brookings Discussion Paper (Washington, D.C.: The Brookings Institution, 1983).

37. Kendrick, "The Implications of Growth Accounting Models," in Hulten and Sawhill, eds., *The Legacy of Reaganomics*.

TABLE 23

Overview of Estimated Impacts of the Reagan Administration's
Policies on Long-Term Economic Growth

	Percentage Change in Real Output by 1990[a]	
	Lower Bound	Upper Bound
Capital formation	−2.8	+1.2
Labor supply	+0.6	+1.8
Regulation[b]	0	+1.0
Education and training	−0.4	0
Research and Development	−0.8	+0.4
Total	−3.4	+4.4

Sources: Tables 21 and 22 and Appendix B. For a similar effort, see William D. Nordhaus, "Reaganomics and Economic Growth: A Summing Up," in Hulten and Sawhill, eds., *The Legacy of Reaganomics.*

Notes: These figures were arrived at in the following way:

Capital Formation. We add up the numbers from table 21 and apply a coefficient of 0.3 to translate them into changes in output. The results may be too optimistic, because the positive effects of the tax cuts on investment depend to some extent on the assumption that the required savings will be available.

Labor Supply. We start with Haveman's results, which indicate an increase of between 0.8 and 2.5 percent in the labor supply (table 22). This translates into an increase of 0.6 to 1.8 percent in GNP via a Cobb-Douglas production function in which labor's share of GNP is assumed to be 70 percent.

Regulation. We assume an increase of between 0 and 0.2 percent a year in multifactor productivity for a period of about five years, leading to an increase of 0 to 1 percent in GNP at end of the period. See Gregory B. Christainsen and Robert H. Haveman, "The Reagan Administration's Regulatory Relief Effort and Productivity," in George C. Eads and Michael Fix, eds., *The Reagan Regulatory Strategy: An Assessment* (Washington, D.C.: The Urban Institute Press, 1984), and John W. Kendrick, "The Implications of Growth Accounting Models," in Hulten and Sawhill, eds., *The Legacy of Reaganomics.* These estimates are very sensitive to what one assumes the growth of social regulations would have been under a different administration.

Education and Training. We assume that outlays on education and training as a proportion of GNP are reduced by 0.3 percentage points. In the upper-bound estimate, we assume a 75 percent replacement rate and a 5 percent rate of return to these investments. In the lower-bound estimate we assume a 25 percent replacement rate and a 10 percent rate of return. The returns are assumed to cumulate (at a compound rate) over a ten-year period. See Daniel H. Saks, "Human Resource Consequences of Reagan's Social Policy," Changing Domestic Priorities Discussion Paper (Washington, D.C.: The Urban Institute, 1983); and Schultze, "Alternative Measures of Federal Investment Outlays," in Hulten and Sawhill, eds., *The Legacy of Reaganomics.*

R&D. We assume that outlays on R&D as a proportion of GNP are increased by 0.05 percentage points (mainly by R&D tax credit) in the upper-bound estimate and that the share is decreased by 0.1 percentage points in the lower-bound estimate (mainly because of reductions in nondefense R&D budget outlays). The rate of return in both cases is assumed to be 25 percent (compounded over ten years). See Oliner, Haveman, and David, "Investment in Equipment, Structures, and Research Capital Under the Reagan Tax Acts," March 1983; Schultze, "Alternative Measures of Federal Investment Outlays," in Hulten and Sawhill, eds., *The Legacy of Reaganomics*; Edwin Mansfield, "Public Policy Toward Industrial

tion's policies to this increase is hard to estimate. Some economists believe that the 25 percent incremental R&D tax credit passed as part of ERTA in 1981 has encouraged private R&D spending, which is currently quite strong, whereas others contend that the effects have been small or nonexistent.[38] Total federal outlays for R&D have increased slightly since 1980 but all the increases have been in the defense area; nondefense R&D expenditures are lower than they have been in any recent administration.[39] Thus, the benefits of higher federal expenditures depend on whether one believes there are large technological spillovers from defense into the civilian sector, a matter about which opinions differ.

Summary

Our overall assessment of the effects of Reagan policies on long-term growth is summarized in table 23. As we have indicated all along, there is considerable uncertainty about all these numbers. Nevertheless, they do serve to focus the debate and to put reasonable bounds on the range of likely effects. They also serve as a reminder of how little is really known about the growth process.

With all their flaws, the numbers are still suggestive. They indicate that, under optimistic assumptions, the net impact of a large number of

---

38. Eileen L. Collins, "An Early Assessment of Three R&D Tax Incentives Provided by the Economic Recovery Tax Act of 1981," PRA Report 83-7 (Washington, D.C.: National Science Foundation, 1983). Edwin Mansfield, "Public Policy Toward Industrial Innovation: An International Study of R&D Tax Credits," presented at the Harvard Business School's 75th Anniversary Colloquium on Productivity and Technology (Cambridge, Mass.: Harvard University Press, forthcoming).

39. Nichols, "Federal Spending Priorities and Long-Term Economic Growth," in Hulten and Sawhill, eds., *The Legacy of Reaganomics.*

NOTES TO TABLE 23 (continued)

Innovation: An International Study of R&D Tax Credits," presented at the Harvard Business School's 75th Anniversary Colloquium on Productivity and Technology (Cambridge, Mass.: Harvard University Press, forthcoming); Barry P. Bosworth, "Capital Formation, Technology, and Economic Policy," Brookings Discussion Paper (Washington, D.C.: The Brookings Institution, 1983); Eileen L. Collins, "An Early Assessment of Three R&D Tax Incentives provided by the Economic Recovery Tax Act of 1981," PRA Report 83-7 (Washington, D.C.: National Science Foundation, 1983).

a. This is the total impact on the level of output. If the effects take place gradually over, say, ten years, then the *annual* growth rate would be raised (lowered) by one-tenth as much.

b. Effects on market productivity only. The greater social costs that might accompany this shift are ignored in this calculation.

FIGURE 14

THE IMPACT OF THE REAGAN ADMINISTRATION'S POLICIES
ON POTENTIAL GNP

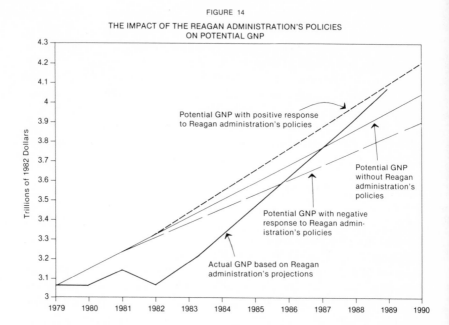

SOURCE: Office of Management and Budget, *Budget of the
United States Government, Fiscal Year 1985* (Washington, D.C.: Government Printing Office, 1984); authors'
calculations.

effects, some negative and some positive, is to increase potential output in
1990 by as much as 4.4 percent. Under more pessimistic assumptions, the
net impact is to decrease potential output by 3.4 percent.[40] If the budget
deficits can be reduced and continuing economic slack or another recession avoided, the net effect would definitely be positive.

Figure 14 compares the growth path of potential GNP (the economy's
capacity to supply goods and services) under these optimistic and pessimistic assumptions with the path that might have been expected without the
Reagan administration's policies. The figure also shows the administration's 1984 forecast of actual GNP (total demand for goods and services).
The administration assumes that the supply of output will rise more or less
in line with our optimistic growth path. If the pessimistic scenario should
prove to be the correct one, and demand grows as forecast, actual GNP will
surpass potential in 1986 and the risk of inflation will increase greatly. If
the administration is right about the growth of potential GNP, we may
really see a return to sustained noninflationary growth.

---

40. In the appendix B, using a somewhat more sophisticated and consistent methodol-
ogy, we obtain similar results: a range of between plus 3.2 percent and minus 2.8 percent.

CHAPTER 5

CONCLUSIONS

In its critique of past economic policy and performance, the Reagan administration properly focused on inflation and inadequate productivity growth as the major problems facing the American economy in 1981. Its diagnosis of the causes of these problems was, however, overly simple. Excessive emphasis was placed on the need to reduce the size of government, when what was really needed was a reappraisal of whether existing programs were providing benefits commensurate with their costs. Tax cuts and regulatory relief were justified as vital for restoring productivity, when their likely effects, although in the right direction, were more modest than what the administration was suggesting. Finally, monetary restraint was necessary if inflation was to be reduced significantly, but the public was not told that the costs of lowering inflation would be high. Although many economists voiced these objections at the time, the optimism inherent in the Reagan administration's program was seductive. People were willing to suspend their disbelief in the hope that the president's economic recovery program would work.

The greatest success for the administration has been on the inflation front, but here it must share credit with the Federal Reserve. Moreover, it was a good time to be president: oil, food, and import price movements all helped inflation fall, making policy look even more effective than it was.

A recession in 1981 and 1982 was all but inevitable. However, an easier monetary policy combined with a tighter fiscal policy would have produced a milder recession that would have, on average, made each person in the country between $500 and $600 richer by the end of 1983. Although inflation would not have come down so fast or so far, it would nevertheless have declined substantially. There would have been more growth in housing and net exports and less in consumption.

Whether the Reagan administration's policies have been good for growth is debatable. Since much of the president's program was aimed at

101

improving standards of living, not immediately but over the longer run, we would like to be more definitive on this critical issue. However, economists have trouble fully explaining the economic growth process, and much of the evidence cited in chapter 4, while the best currently available, simply cannot support such a judgment.

One thing is abundantly clear from the evidence: no administration can have a major impact on the economy's long-run growth rate. Almost any conceivable policy turns out to have small, usually temporary, effects. Increasing real GNP by 5 percent at the end of ten years, or by an average of about half a point a year, as table 23 demonstrates, would be the most that reasonably could be hoped for. Conversely, reducing the rate of growth by a comparable amount is about the worst outcome that reasonably could be imagined. Whether positive or negative, the effects almost surely lie within this range. Exaggerating the effectiveness of its policies is a political disease that this administration has shared with almost all others. Supply-side economics is no more a panacea for our economic ills than was demand-side economics at an earlier point in our history.

Nevertheless, the Reagan administration has, in our view, left three significant legacies for the 1980s. The first is a much lower rate of inflation. The second is large budget deficits; unless current policies are changed, these deficits will cumulate to $1.3 trillion by 1990. The deficits are the major reason for our somewhat pessimistic conclusions about long-term growth. Our calculations suggest that almost any action undertaken to reduce these deficits will have a positive impact on growth.

The third legacy of the Reagan administration is a less tangible, but possibly important, shift in expectations about what government should or will do.[1] The administration has fostered this shift mostly by virtue of its rhetoric and its ideology, although its stance is also symbolically manifest in its tax and regulatory policies and in its willingness to tolerate a long recession. This change in ideological climate does not yet seem to have discernibly affected wage- and price-setting practices or, for that matter, other kinds of economic behavior.[2] Yet public opinion surveys suggest that the president has struck a responsive chord, and messages from the Rose Garden about the importance of entrepreneurship and individual initiative may yet have an impact on the way managers and workers behave and, perhaps, on the economy's efficiency and productivity. The inability of economists to adequately explain the long-term rise and fall of national economies could rest on just such intangibles.

---

1. For a similar set of observations, see William D. Nordhaus, "Reaganomics and Economic Growth: A Summing Up," in Hulten and Sawhill, *The Legacy of Reaganomics*.

2. Blinder, "The Message in the Models," in Hulten and Sawhill, eds., *The Legacy of Reaganomics*.

APPENDIX A

This appendix contains a description of the alternatives to actual policies that we have used in the simulations discussed in chapters 2 and 3.[1] We have made our alternative fiscal policy more restrictive than actual policy has been in order to eliminate large structural deficits. Our alternative monetary policy is less restrictive, not only to offset the additional fiscal restraint, but also to provide greater overall stimulus in order to avoid a recession as severe as the one we experienced.

Fiscal Policy

Our alternative fiscal policy assumes an overall budget stance that keeps the high-employment federal government budget in approximate balance throughout the simulation period (1981–1988).[2] In contrast to actual policies, we assume slower real growth in defense spending, fewer cuts in nondefense expenditures, and smaller tax cuts.

Defense Spending. Although there was bipartisan support for the increase in defense spending begun in the Carter administration, we assume that a different administration would not have supported a defense buildup as large as the Reagan administration's buildup. In particular, we assume real defense spending growth of 5 percent in 1982, 4 percent in 1983, and 3 percent in 1984 and thereafter. Actual growth in defense spending was 7 percent in 1982 and 1983 and is estimated to be 6 percent in 1984 and 5 percent thereafter in our simulation of the Reagan administration's policies.

Nondefense Spending. The real levels of three broad, federal government, nondefense spending categories—nondefense purchases of goods and services, transfers to persons, and grants-in-aid to state and local governments—were specified so that, given our real defense spending growth path and our alternative tax policy (discussed later), the high-employment budget is kept in near balance. These levels are broadly consistent with the baseline projections made by the Congressional Budget Office (CBO) in 1981, hence they assume no substantial cuts from pre-Reagan policy lev-

---

[1] Simulations of economic policy were done using the Data Resources, Inc. (DRI), quarterly econometric forecasting model.

[2] At high employment, the deficit or surplus never exceeds 1 percent of GNP.

els. Real spending in these categories is higher than spending under the Reagan administration's policies.[3]

Transfers to Persons.   With the exception of Social Security and Supplemental Security Income programs (which changed as part of the Social Security Amendments of 1983 and which we assume would have been enacted no matter who was president), we assume that transfer programs would have provided benefits based on 1980 law.

Grants-in-Aid.   Although government activity at the state and local levels is not under the control of any administration, the effects of economic and budget policies at the federal level are likely to induce responsive policy decisions. For example, the decisions since 1981 by eighteen states to raise their personal income taxes were undoubtedly influenced by the decline in grants-in-aid under the Reagan administration's policies and by the recession in 1981 and 1982. Because our alternative fiscal policy assumes fewer cuts in grants-in-aid and because a milder recession in 1981 and 1982 is one result of our alternative policies, we assume that state and local governments do not raise their taxes to such a degree.

Tax Policy.   General concern about the effects of inflation in increasing taxes as a share of income would probably have produced some kind of tax cut in 1981 no matter who was president. Our alternative tax policy assumes that personal income tax rates are indexed for inflation beginning in the fourth quarter of 1981. We assume no business tax cut. Given our concern with limiting the size of the budget deficit, any cut in business taxes would have required a smaller personal income tax cut or a reduction in spending elsewhere. However, if we had assumed a business tax cut, the differential stimulus to business investment that we now ascribe to the Reagan administration's policies would be correspondingly smaller. We assume that the changes in payroll taxes enacted as part of the Social Security reforms and the gas tax increase enacted as a part of the public works jobs program would have occurred whoever was president.

Monetary Policy

The rate of growth of M1 in our simulation of an easier monetary policy combined with actual fiscal policy was as fast as the model would allow in 1981 in order to get the economy to high employment as quickly as possible. The rate of growth of M1 in the easier monetary policy/tighter fiscal policy simulation was somewhat slower and was constrained by consider-

---

[3] We did not make specific assumptions regarding the remaining nondefense spending categories—transfer to foreigners, net interest paid, and subsidies less current surplus of government enterprises—but interest outlays turn out to be lower because the federal deficit and interest rates are lower.

TABLE A.1

Economic Performance Indicators under Four Policy Alternatives, 1981–1988

	1981	1982	1983	1984	1985	1986	1987	1988
I. *Actual Policies*								
Real GNP (billions of 1982 $)	3,132.0	3,073.2	3,176.4	3,352.3	3,465.7	3,566.8	3,677.5	3,806.0
Change (%)	2.6	−1.9	3.4	5.5	3.4	2.9	3.1	3.5
Inflation rate (CPI)	10.3	6.2	3.2	4.9	4.8	5.2	5.6	5.9
Unemployment rate (civilian)	7.6	9.7	9.6	7.6	7.2	7.3	7.3	7.1
Three-month Treasury bill rate	14.0	10.6	8.6	8.8	9.5	9.7	9.4	9.2
II. *Easier Monetary, Tighter Fiscal Policies*								
Real GNP (billions of 1982 $)	3,218.0	3,262.4	3,412.8	3,520.5	3,641.6	3,770.2	3,883.3	4,019.3
Change (%)	4.1	1.4	4.6	3.2	3.4	3.5	3.0	3.5
Inflation rate (CPI)	10.6	7.2	4.7	6.4	6.4	7.2	7.5	7.8
Unemployment rate (civilian)	7.2	8.0	7.3	6.2	6.1	6.1	6.1	6.0
Three-month Treasury bill rate	7.0	4.8	5.4	5.4	4.1	4.8	4.6	5.6
III. *Easier Monetary, Actual Fiscal Policies*								
Real GNP (billions of 1982 $)	3,247.9	3,355.7	3,486.0	3,576.8	3,691.1	3,809.2	3,950.9	4,086.5
Change (%)	4.6	3.3	3.9	2.6	3.2	3.2	3.7	3.4
Inflation rate (CPI)	10.7	7.6	5.3	6.6	6.4	7.1	7.7	7.8
Unemployment rate (civilian)	7.1	7.2	6.6	6.1	6.0	6.1	6.0	6.0
Three-month Treasury bill rate	5.9	3.4	7.7	5.9	6.7	6.2	6.8	6.3
IV. *Actual Monetary, Tighter Fiscal Policies*								
Real GNP (billions of 1982 $)	3,128.7	3,070.4	3,155.6	3,316.0	3,431.4	3,530.7	3,646.0	3,782.7
Change (%)	2.5	−1.9	2.8	5.1	3.5	2.9	3.3	3.8
Inflation rate (CPI)	10.3	6.2	3.2	4.7	4.7	5.2	5.6	6.1
Unemployment rate (civilian)	7.6	9.7	9.8	7.9	7.5	7.4	7.3	6.9
Three-month Treasury bill rate	14.0	10.4	7.4	6.6	6.8	6.3	5.4	5.4

Source: Authors' simulations based on DRI model.

TABLE A.2

Monetary and Fiscal Policy Alternatives, 1981–1988

	1981	1982	1983	1984	1985	1986	1987	1988
I. *Actual Policies*								
	(Percentage)							
M1 growth	5.1	8.9	10.0	6.4	6.4	5.8	5.6	5.6
Receipts/GNP	21.2	20.1	19.5	19.5	19.6	19.7	19.8	20.2
Expenditures/GNP	23.3	24.9	25.0	24.4	24.7	25.0	25.1	25.1
Deficit/GNP	−2.1	−4.8	−5.5	−4.9	−5.1	−5.3	−5.4	−4.9
... at high employment[a]	−0.6	−1.8	−2.7	−3.1	−3.5	−3.7	−3.6	−3.3
	(Billions of current dollars)							
Receipts	627.0	617.4	644.3	712.4	775.7	842.0	920.1	1,027.9
Personal	298.6	304.7	296.0	314.5	344.5	375.9	414.1	460.0
Corporate profits	67.5	46.4	59.9	71.1	75.0	79.1	86.5	92.8
Other[b]	260.9	266.3	288.4	326.8	356.2	387.0	419.5	475.1
Expenditures	689.1	764.4	826.2	890.7	976.2	1,070.0	1,169.4	1,278.1
Defense purchases	154.0	179.4	200.1	222.5	248.8	275.5	305.9	340.1
Nondefense purchases	75.2	79.3	75.0	77.4	93.7	101.0	107.5	114.5
Transfers to persons	280.9	314.8	338.8	353.8	376.2	411.0	442.9	478.9
Grants-in-aid to state and local governments	87.9	83.9	86.5	93.0	101.3	108.0	116.5	126.0
Net interest paid	73.1	84.9	96.4	114.9	132.6	153.1	175.1	195.8
Other[c]	18.0	22.1	29.4	29.1	23.6	21.4	21.5	22.8
Deficit (−) or surplus	−62.1	−147.0	−181.9	−178.3	−200.5	−228.0	−249.2	−250.3
... at high employment[a]	−19.1	−61.4	−95.8	−120.8	−145.8	−165.1	−177.9	−176.3

II. *Easier Monetary,*
   Tighter Fiscal Policies

(Percentage)

M1 growth	10.0	10.1	9.9	6.1	8.1	7.1	6.9	6.6
Receipts/GNP	21.4	21.4	21.9	22.2	22.3	22.1	21.9	22.1
Expenditures/GNP	22.6	22.9	22.4	22.5	22.4	22.1	21.9	21.8
Deficit/GNP	-1.2	-1.5	-0.5	-0.3	-0.1	0.0	0.0	0.3
... at high employment[a]	-0.1	-0.1	0.4	0.3	0.5	0.5	0.6	1.0

(Billions of current dollars)

Receipts	643.3	696.8	790.5	873.3	964.0	1,061.0	1,163.5	1,310.2
Personal	300.5	326.7	356.0	385.1	420.2	461.6	509.5	570.0
Corporate profits	78.2	90.3	124.1	136.6	154.1	166.3	176.2	188.3
Other[b]	264.6	279.8	310.4	351.6	389.7	433.1	477.8	551.9
Expenditures	679.3	747.6	810.3	886.3	969.0	1,062.4	1,165.6	1,290.3
Defense purchases	154.4	178.1	195.7	214.2	237.9	263.6	292.0	325.1
Nondefense purchases	75.3	80.8	83.0	91.0	110.2	120.7	131.0	142.6
Transfers to persons	279.9	316.0	344.2	379.2	411.3	457.2	503.5	557.8
Grants-in-aid to state and local governments	89.5	93.6	99.3	108.1	120.6	132.4	148.3	167.2
Net interest paid	62.1	56.9	58.6	64.8	65.5	67.1	69.4	74.8
Other[c]	18.1	22.1	29.5	29.0	23.5	21.4	21.4	22.8
Deficit (−) or surplus	-36.0	-50.8	-19.8	-13.1	-5.0	-1.4	-2.0	19.9
... at high employment[a]	-4.4	-2.9	13.7	13.8	22.1	26.1	35.3	59.1

III. *Easier Monetary,*
   Actual Fiscal Policies

(Percentage)

M1 growth	11.2	11.4	8.5	6.4	7.4	7.7	7.1	7.6
Receipts/GNP	21.3	20.8	20.3	19.9	19.9	19.9	20.0	20.3
Expenditures/GNP	22.4	21.8	21.6	21.7	21.9	21.9	21.6	21.5
Deficit/GNP	-1.1	-1.0	-1.3	-1.8	-2.0	-2.0	-1.6	-1.2
... at high employment[a]	-0.1	-0.2	-0.9	-1.3	-1.5	-1.4	-1.0	-0.6

TABLE A.2 (continued)

MONETARY AND FISCAL POLICY ALTERNATIVES, 1981–1988

	1981	1982	1983	1984	1985	1986	1987	1988
	(Billions of current dollars)							
Receipts	643.9	699.0	750.5	804.0	880.1	970.8	1,089.9	1,234.8
Personal	301.6	330.1	334.4	349.8	390.5	438.3	501.2	571.7
Corporate profits	76.5	82.5	97.7	92.8	88.9	88.6	96.1	95.4
Other[b]	265.8	286.4	318.4	361.4	400.7	443.9	492.6	567.7
Expenditures	676.3	731.0	799.1	874.9	968.0	1,068.9	1,180.1	1,308.5
Defense purchases	154.5	182.3	206.7	232.6	262.9	294.8	332.6	376.6
Nondefense purchases	75.4	80.8	77.7	81.5	99.9	109.3	118.6	129.0
Transfers to persons	279.5	309.3	337.8	366.2	396.3	441.2	484.5	534.7
Grants-in-aid to state and local governments	88.1	85.1	89.2	97.2	107.2	115.8	126.8	139.2
Net interest paid	60.7	51.5	58.2	68.2	78.2	86.4	96.2	106.1
Other[c]	18.1	22.0	29.5	29.2	23.5	21.4	21.4	22.9
Deficit (−) or surplus	−32.4	−32.0	−48.7	−70.8	−87.8	−98.1	−90.3	−73.7
... at high employment[a]	−4.7	−7.8	−35.7	−55.3	−68.1	−69.6	−58.2	−36.2
IV. *Actual Monetary, Tighter Fiscal Policies*	(Percentage)							
M1 growth	5.1	8.9	10.0	6.5	6.3	5.8	5.7	5.7
Receipts/GNP	21.4	21.1	21.5	22.0	22.3	22.2	22.0	22.3
Expenditures/GNP	23.4	25.2	25.4	24.9	24.8	24.8	24.5	24.2
Deficit/GNP	−2.0	−4.1	−3.9	−2.9	−2.5	−2.6	−2.5	−1.9
... at high employment[a]	−0.4	−1.0	−0.7	−0.7	−0.7	−0.8	−0.7	−0.4

(Billions of current dollars)

Receipts	632.8	647.3	709.0	793.5	869.5	934.5	1,012.6	1,125.6
Personal	300.1	316.2	332.0	358.7	386.2	414.2	448.0	489.6
Corporate profits	72.1	65.0	90.2	111.7	131.5	138.4	149.5	162.9
Other[b]	260.6	266.1	286.8	323.1	351.8	381.9	415.1	473.1
Expenditures	690.4	773.7	835.2	897.6	967.4	1,043.5	1,125.1	1,220.3
Defense purchases	154.0	175.9	190.9	206.3	226.4	247.5	270.4	296.5
Nondefense purchases	75.1	79.7	80.8	87.1	104.0	112.2	119.7	127.9
Transfers to persons	281.1	319.5	346.0	370.8	393.9	429.3	463.9	504.3
Grants-in-aid to state and local governments	89.3	92.6	97.1	104.2	114.7	124.1	137.1	152.7
Net interest paid	72.8	83.8	91.1	100.0	104.9	109.1	112.6	116.0
Other[c]	18.1	22.2	29.3	29.2	23.5	21.3	21.4	22.9
Deficit (−) or surplus	−57.7	−126.4	−126.2	−104.1	−97.9	−109.0	−112.5	−94.7
... at high employment[a]	−13.1	−34.5	−24.9	−28.3	−27.6	−33.6	−33.8	−21.1

SOURCE: Authors' simulations based on DRI model.

a. Assumes high-employment unemployment rate of 6.0 percent in 1981 and 1982, 5.9 percent between 1983 and 1986, and 5.8 percent between 1987 and 1988.

b. Includes indirect business tax and nontax accruals and contributions for social insurance.

c. Includes net transfer payments to foreigners and subsidies less current surplus of government enterprises.

ations of what might be acceptable to an administration more concerned with unemployment than the Reagan administration but still hesitant to expand the economy as rapidly as possible.

Results

Tables A.1 and A.2 show some of the important performance and policy variables for the four simulations discussed in chapters 2 and 3. Section I in each table shows these data for our simulation of the Reagan administration's policies assuming no policy change in the 1984–1988 period, while sections II–IV show data for the alternative monetary and fiscal policies described in the text.

APPENDIX B

ESTIMATING THE IMPACTS OF THE REAGAN ADMINISTRATION'S POLICIES ON ECONOMIC GROWTH AND THE LEVEL OF REAL GNP OVER THE 1980s

The model used to simulate the impacts of various policies is specified as follows:

$$GNP_t = AK_t \cdot {}^3L_t \cdot {}^7$$
$$A = (1 + r)^t$$
$$K_t = K_{t-1} + NI_t$$
$$L_t = (1 + n)L_{t-1}$$
$$NI_t = sGNP_t$$

GNP growth is determined by the growth of capital (K), labor (L), and technological change (A) using a Cobb-Douglas production function. The gross capital stock is augmented by net investment (NI) each period, and the level of net investment equals the net savings ratio (s) times *GNP* in the current period. The savings rate (s) together with the rate of technological change (r) and the growth of the (full-time-equivalent) labor force (n) are specified exogenously.

In the policy simulations, the values of each variable are specified as follows in the base (control) simulation:

$$s = .06$$
$$r = .01$$
$$n = .015$$
$$K_o = 270$$
$$L_o = 63$$
$$GNP_o = 100$$

These values are consistent with evidence that the net savings rate has been in the neighborhood of 6 percent for much of the post-World War II period, the labor force is projected to grow by about 1.5 percent during the 1980s, 1 percent seems as good a guess as any for the growth of multifactor

111

productivity over this period, and the gross capital-to-output ratio is about 2.7.[1]

Shifts in policy are assumed to affect s, r, or n, respectively. We choose to focus on the impact of these assumed shifts on the level of real potential *GNP* five and ten years after the change.[2] To the extent that the economy is operating well below its potential over this period, we cannot assume that these gains in potential will be realized.

The results of the simulations are shown in table B.1. Section I of the table shows the effects on *GNP* of assumed shifts in each of our key growth parameters, holding other parameters constant. Section II shows the effects of a simultaneous shift in all the parameters under both pessimistic and optimistic scenarios. We consider the pessimistic scenario to be about the worst that could be expected as a result of the Reagan administration's

TABLE B.1

SIMULATION RESULTS

I. Results from Changing One Parameter at a Time

Parameter and Assumed Value	Percentage Change in GNP by Year 5	Percentage Change in GNP by Year 10
$s = .05$	−0.4	−0.9
$s = .04$	−0.9	−1.9
$n = .016$	0.3	0.6
$n = .017$	0.6	1.3
$n = .018$	0.8	1.9
$r = .009$	−0.4	−0.9
$r = .011$	0.4	0.9
$r = .012$	0.8	1.9
$r = .015$	2.0	4.7

II. Results from Simultaneous Simulation

Parameter and Assumed Value	Percentage Change in GNP by Year 5	Percentage Change in GNP by Year 10
Pessimistic scenario ($s = .04$, $n = .015$, $r = .009$)	−1.3	−2.8
Optimistic scenario ($s = .06$, $n = .017$, $r = .012$)	+1.4	+3.2

---

1. According to the BEA, the gross stock of residential and nonresidential capital was \$4 trillion (in 1972 dollars) in 1982. This compares with a *GNP* of \$1.5 trillion (in 1972 dollars).

2. Strictly speaking, year 1 is treated as the base year, so the results represent four and nine years of change, respectively.

policy changes and the optimistic scenario to be about the best that could be expected.

Briefly, the reasoning behind these two scenarios is as follows: under the pessimistic scenario, the saving rate falls from 6 percent to 4 percent, mainly as the result of the deficits, but the effect of the deficits is exacerbated by the 1981–1982 recession and any continuing slack on capital formation. These effects swamp, or crowd out, any positive effects from the business tax cuts. The growth of labor is assumed to be unaffected by the personal tax cuts, and multifactor productivity growth drops by 0.1 percentage points per year (from 1 to 0.9) as the result of the cutbacks in federal spending on education, training, and civilian R&D. Hence, on average, the rate of growth of *GNP* is reduced by slightly more than 0.3 percentage points per year (from, say, 4 percent to 3.7 percent) for nine years, so that the level of real *GNP* is 2.8 percentage points lower at the end of the period.

Under the optimistic scenario, the saving rate remains unchanged under the assumption that deficits will be reduced soon and that whatever structural deficit remains might be offset by an increase in private saving or by a shift of available saving into more productive forms of investment as the result of the Feldstein twist and the administration's elimination of the most marginal and inefficient forms of public investment. The labor supply grows at a rate of 1.7 percent instead of 1.5 percent a year as a result of the Reagan tax and transfer program cuts. And multifactor productivity growth increases by 0.2 percentage points per year (from 1 to 1.2), mainly as the result of the regulatory relief program and the R&D tax credit. The result is an increase in the annual growth rate of *GNP* of a little over 0.3 percentage points per year, which yields a 3.2 percent higher level of output at the end of the decade.